Laughing Matters

Selected Columns
by Humorist
Pam Robbins

Laughing Matters:
Selected Columns
by Humorist Pam Robbins

By Pam Robbins

Published by:
Global Business Perspectives Inc.
310 South Street
Northampton, MA 01060 USA
413-586-8588

First Edition, First Printing 1998

*Printed in the
United States of America*

*Library of Congress
Cataloging-in-Publication Data*

*Robbins, Pam
    Laughing Matters: Selected
Columns by Humorist Pam
Robbins / by Pam Robbins -1st Ed.*

ISBN 0-9667357-0-6

1. Humor

98-88047 CIP

To my mother
for most of all
the laughter

Acknowledgments

This project had more people involved than a Wagnerian opera, and I am grateful to all of them.

In particular, I'd like to thank Annie Emanuelli who prepared the manuscript and ancillary materials; Ellie Cook, Tzivia Gover and Gloria Girouard who volunteered to proofread; T. Lak who designed the book; Peggy Moran, who designed the Web page; and George Phillips, who provided the cover drawing (and made it thinner when I asked.)

I'm also grateful to everyone who spurred, soothed and encouraged me through assorted crises and helped in tangible and intangible ways at any phase of this undertaking. They include: Ruth Danckert, Evie Goldich, the Rev. Mary Lewis Webb, Roe Schmidt, Barry Steeves, Karen Ahearn, Suzanne Wilson, Cate Chant, and all of my colleagues and friends at the *Daily Hampshire Gazette*.

It was in the *Gazette's* weekly magazine, *Hampshire Life,* that these columns first found a home. I am indebted therefore to the paper's publishers, Charles DeRose and Peter DeRose, to its editor, Jim Foudy, and to *Hampshire Life's* editor, Debra Scherban.

And I especially want to thank Gregory Sandler of Global Business Perspectives, who not only proposed this book, but also actually made it happen—not that I ever had a single doubt.

Foreword

To write the foreword to a book, it seems to me, three conditions are necessary.

You must know or at least be acquainted with the author; you must appreciate, even admire, the author's work, and you must have read and enjoyed the book in question and be willing to recommend it.

Happily, in this case, all three criteria are met.

I have known Pam Robbins for most of her life, though we occasionally lose touch with each other. While I find her annoying at times, I also think she is very amusing. In fact, it has been said that no one laughs harder at her jokes than I do. True enough.

Moreover, I have read every word of this book, which consists of 34 columns culled from some 150 produced over several years, and I could not have written it better.

I hope you find Pam Robbins as funny as I do.

Pam Robbins

1998

Table of Contents

Resolutions: One Is Fun But Eight Are Great

The custom of making just one New Year's resolution each year seems to me to be flawed at the very heart of it. Once you break the resolution, which you surely will, you become an immediate and total failure, at least in your own eyes.

That's why I like to make many resolutions, so that I can fail by degrees over a period of time. Much easier to take.

It is in that spirit that I plan to make eight resolutions for this year. I share them with you here in the hopes of inspiring you to do likewise.

Resolution #1: To write it down and bring it with me.

For me, this will be the year of the list. I am determined to write down everything I am supposed to do and when I am supposed to do it, so that I can't possibly forget.

The need for me to do this is greater than ever, as evidenced by the fact that I recently had to write myself several notes to accomplish a single task.

First note: "Send check to Betsy."

Second note: "Look up Betsy's address."

Third note: "Mail check to Betsy."

Fourth note: "Buy stamps."

As you can see, I actually have made a pretty good start on this list-making business, except that I usually leave the list somewhere and can't remember what was on it.

That translates into return trips to the grocery store, apologies for missed appointments, and lots of lost time.

The capper was the day I brought an ailing family member to the doctor's office. Since this doctor has his office in the bowels of the least-accessible building in this hemisphere, it took some doing to get her there. But I did — only to have the receptionist greet me with an air of consternation.

"Um, your appointment is at 1:30," she said. I noticed then that there was no one else in the waiting room, which I took to be a good sign.

I also noticed, through the glass window, that the doctor was putting on a hat and coat, which I took to be a bad sign. Either the heating plant had failed, or he was going somewhere.

"I'm 15 minutes early," I said somewhat testily.

"Well," she said very patiently. "It's 12:15. You're actually an hour and 15 minutes early. We're closing for lunch."

Let's say that the hour spent with my loved one in a locked office with lights dimmed and dumb music playing was an experience I'll cherish, but wouldn't care to repeat.

So in addition to writing it all down, I resolve to bring the list with me — and to buy a watch with really BIG hands.

Resolution #2: To use fewer clichés or die trying.

As a former coworker used to say, "Clichés are not my cup of tea." But I resort to them too often in a pinch and I resolve to stop — and there's no time like the present, so to speak.

Resolution #3: To continue my battle against the all-too-prevalent error in sentence construction whereby one says, for example: "Having been in bed for several months, doctors decided to induce labor."

This suggests two things: If the doctors had gotten out of bed sooner, maybe things would have gone better for the patient. And the person using that sentence must have skipped school the day that antecedents were taught.

Resolution #4: To refrain from uttering or writing the word "butt" unless I am discussing a cut of pork.

There will be no mention of kicking butt, sitting on one's butt or getting one's butt here or there. While I'm at it, I will make no puns on the other kind of butt, as in "Smoking law enforced - no ifs, ands or butts." I promise.

Resolution #5: To watch as much television as is humanly possible in an effort to balance out the people who like to brag about never watching any. P.S. What do you people DO?

Resolution #6: To read one Newsweek before the next one arrives.

I was going to resolve to read Newsweek before I read TV Guide, but... see Resolution #5 above.

Resolution #7: To cut my fat gram consumption in half, which means eating 50 grams before noon and 50 after noon.

Then there is **Resolution #8**, my major, annual, life-changing resolution.

One year I turned to a colleague and said: "This year I am going to be a nicer person. I'm not going to make fun of anyone."

Are you familiar with the expression belly laugh?

Every December since then, I have said the same thing to her and elicited the same reaction. She goes home and tells her husband, then reports back to me about his reaction. I think the phrase she uses is "cracked up."

Am I ever really going to be any nicer? What do you think? But I like to do my part to make their holiday season merry and bright. So I resolve to make the same resolution again next year.

What the heck, talk is cheap.

Somebody Called,
But I Was Out Somewhere

I'm thinking of calling a private investigator. I need to track down Somebody.

I don't mean anybody, I mean Somebody.

I'm using Somebody in this case as a proper name because I'm sure he is a specific individual. I also am sure he's a he — because no she would plague another woman the way Somebody has been plaguing me.

This has been going on too long. And I think it's time to put a stop to it.

It's going to be hard to explain to a PI, however. I have no data to offer: no address, no Social Security number, no photo. I can offer only a history of Somebody's behavior. I hope that will supply enough clues.

It began a few years ago. I don't remember exactly how. Maybe Somebody forgot to tighten the lid on the peanut butter jar, and when somebody else picked it up by the lid, the jar dropped and broke.

That may have been the first time I heard it. "Somebody didn't cap the peanut butter jar."

Or maybe Somebody forgot the house key and had to break into the house.

Whatever it was, I'm sure I looked around and saw no one else in the room.

I've looked around a lot of times since then. There's never anybody else in the room. If you were to search all the rooms, in fact, you would find no one except two irritated human beings, one of them mumbling that Somebody did such and such.

Sometimes the second person can be heard to mumble, "Well, it wasn't me."

And then the first person says, "Well, Somebody did it."

This exchange usually seems to satisfy both people, in an odd sort of way, and they let the matter drop.

Clearly, when there's trouble, Somebody has had a hand in it. No question about that.

The way I see it, Somebody has a key to my house — or knows a secret way to enter and exit without being seen, because he comes and goes, leaving his mark almost daily.

Over the years, Somebody has neglected to put the cap on the toothpaste, the butter in the refrigerator, and the trash in the barrel.

Somebody sometimes forgets to get gas when the gauge is on empty and never remembers to replace the roll of toilet tissue.

Somebody has returned the library books late, left the keys in the car and dumped a whole can of pepper in the sauce.

This is the same Somebody who frequently turns off the answering machine when it's supposed to be on, or eats the last Fig Newton, or leaves the new bag of cat litter in the trunk of the car.

I'm puzzled by the fact that Somebody always seems to be wreaking havoc in my life, yet manages to be in other places at the exact same time.

I know this because people tell me.

"Somebody forgot to lock my car the other night and

my radio got stolen." When I ask who was in the car that day, the complainant gets testy.

"Just me. But I ALWAYS lock my car. So Somebody must have done it earlier in the week."

This is delivered in a tone that broaches no contradiction.

The other possibility is that there is more than one Somebody, a whole legion of Somebodies, perhaps. In various places Somebody may go by various names. A friend says that when she was growing up, for example, her stepfather used to say it was 'the little ghost" who left the lights on.

So it seems reasonable to me that Somebody either is that little ghost, or is in league with it.

I don't think Somebody spends as much time in houses with lots of children. In those households, there is always a sibling who might have done it — or failed to do it, as the case may be.

But even if your brother did it, Somebody probably put him up to it.

In my own home, I waver between blaming Somebody myself, and staunchly defending him.

A recent exchange went something like this:

"Somebody took my tweezers."

"No, Somebody didn't take your tweezers. You probably put them somewhere and don't remember where."

"No, I didn't. Somebody used them and didn't put them back."

The argument escalated until both parties were about to kill each other.

Then both of them realized that there was no point in being miffed at each other. Obviously, neither of them was at fault.

But Somebody had better bring those tweezers back — and soon.

Uncommon Ways To Conquer the Common Cold

In the past few weeks, I've seen more parched lips and fevered brows than Lawrence of Arabia. It's the cold and flu season and people around me are dropping like the extras in a World War II movie.

As I struggle with my own ongoing hypochondria, I find it inspiring that despite their agony, all of these people have secret remedies they are willing to share with others. Some are mundane — such as minestrone soup, hot showers, vitamin C and extra blankets.

But one man told me that when he has a cold, he waits till the temperature gets into the 30s, then runs five or six miles, comes home and drinks a bottle of stout. He claims this accelerates the process: A cold that normally would last five days works its way through his system in five hours.

It sounds like a good plan, assuming the temperature gets out of the teens during the week you are sick, and assuming you can get out of bed and remain upright long enough to carry out the rest of the steps.

An old friend of mine swore by hot toddies. She made

me one many years ago when I was suffering from laryngitis. I didn't care much for it, but it did cheer me up. Actually, she made me two hot toddies and since I am a teetotaler, they hit me so hard that I laughed uproariously — albeit silently — for several hours.

I've never had another one, but I still smile when people say hot toddy.

One co-worker swore some months ago that she had found a no-fail regimen to prevent colds from gaining the upper hand. It had something to do with consuming a concoction of water and orange juice — mixed in a 5-gallon drum, I think she said — swallowing some analgesics — round not lozenge-shaped — and going to bed very early.

This remedy seemed promising at the time. But it seems less so since that particular woman has come down with the flu.

Well, she is telling people she went out to dinner and the host sabotaged her by sneaking too much butter into the sweet potatoes. Maybe so, but it sounds a lot like the flu to me.

In any case, she feels poorly and that's too bad, but it's her own fault.

This woman takes good care of herself. Too good. I keep explaining to her that clean living is all right, in moderation. But when your lifestyle is overly wholesome, your body gets spoiled. It loses its ability to make adjustments and process pollutants.

All that good food and exercise creates an environment in which a simple sickness has no competition and, therefore, can thrive.

It's as if the germs look around at their pristine surroundings, assume they are being cultivated in a test tube, and obligingly flourish.

I can't convince my friend of this, however. And when she is well, she no doubt will argue that her overall fine condition helped her recover more quickly than she would have otherwise.

Since it is impossible to prove her wrong, or myself right, I'll leave her to her own devices.

When I get a cold myself, I favor remedies that come from the food family — garlic, marinara sauce and plenty of chocolate.

My independent research suggests that in a normally healthy person, no common cold virus or basic flu strain can coexist with high levels of chocolate in the bloodstream.

Chocolate is nature's own combination of proven ingredients: One element bolsters the other. The caffeine speeds the sugar through your poor, sick body and speeds up healing.

Oh sure, you won't see my theory in any medical books, but test it yourself. When you feel a cold coming on, eat some chocolate. See if you don't feel better.

If that doesn't work, you've let it go too far.

Your best bet in that case is to drink two hot toddies and laugh yourself silly.

New Friends, a Glimpse of the Future-by Phone

I fell asleep with the TV on the other night, and when I awakened, there was a woman on the screen inviting me — and whomever else was watching around 2 a.m. — to call her if we felt the need to talk.

Well, as it happened, I did feel the need to talk. But I didn't call. Somehow I never feel much like confiding in a woman who brushes all her tresses over one shoulder and wears an outfit chosen by Madonna's wardrobe mistress.

Beyond that, even in my semi-comatose state, I realized this was just another 900-number ad. So I ignored her.

At first, when these ads began appearing, they were a novelty and I paid some attention. I've found three types interesting from a sociological perspective: the myriad merchandise ads; the ads by women like the aforementioned woman who solicit phone calls from strangers; and the ads for psychics.

The merchandise ads remind me of how many products there are that I wouldn't want for free, but that other people apparently are willing to pay shipping to get.

There are a whole bunch of things you can get by dialing 900 numbers — and most of them are "not available in stores," as they say.

I always find that claim curious. Wouldn't you think that if there really WAS a magic skin-care product, furniture polish or vegetable knife that someone would have hit upon the wacky idea of selling it in a store?

But hey: no harm, no foul. You like to get your sunglasses through the mail, it's fine with me.

More irksome are the pitches by the little band of merry women looking to boost phone bills nationwide.

First of all, is it not a phenomenon that, except for differences in coloring, so many women would look and act so much alike? Who's behind these ads — The Stepford Wives?

Really, all the women in these ads are stick-thin, with more hair than anyone really has a use for. They even have similar voices, or seem to, since none of them speaks much above a whisper.

They also have similar messages, which consist of "Call me" — at the low, low price of $2,019 per minute, or whatever it is — and at least one reason why someone should.

The reasons they state are along the lines of friendship, understanding, a friendly ear and the like. I have two problems with that. First, I wouldn't trust these people to give me directions to the nearest emergency room, so why would I confide in them? Secondly, I don't believe it's female bonding they have in mind.

So I'm cynical; sue me. It's just an opinion.

The third category of 900-number ads really drives me nuts.

"Call your personal psychic," these ads promise, and he or she will help you to make major life choices.

These ads usually show someone holding a phone and saying, "I met this guy. What do you think? Do we have a future together?"

Meanwhile, a voice-over is saying, "Talk to a live psychic now."

Well, I would agree that if you were interested in speaking to a psychic, a live psychic would be your best bet. Besides, if you were able to talk to a dead psychic, you'd have some pretty remarkable powers of your own and probably wouldn't need an intermediary.

But I still hate these ads.

It's not that I'm a skeptic. I'm sure many people have powers the rest of us don't begin to understand, and psychic ability is among them.

The thing is: If you had been born with a rare gift — to divine the future or commune with spirits, say, or to bend spoons by just looking at them — would you be sitting around at the other end of a 900-number?

I know I would. Actually, if I could predict world revolution and natural disasters, I would busy myself pondering whether Julia Roberts will marry again. My Rolodex would include the numbers of all the tabloids in the world. And I absolutely would hire myself out to sit at a console in a big room somewhere, answering calls from people who want to know their lucky numbers.

What a meaningful and rewarding use of such special gifts.

There I'd be, sipping a seltzer and answering the phone.

"Hello, I'm a live psychic," I would say. "I predicted the end of communism. I am also a gifted healer, specializing in PMS and male-pattern baldness. But I have chosen to work for this organization in order to make myself available coast to coast. I also get volume bonuses and pro-rated benefits.

"How can I help you this evening? You want to know your lucky number? Of course I know it. It's 17.

"And mine is 1-900..."

Keeping the State Troopers Entertained

There is no question that state troopers, like all police officers, face danger daily. But their job does have its compensations. Besides getting to wear those nifty uniforms, they also get to observe the stupid way people behave in their presence.

What could be more amusing? If I were a trooper, I'd toss out the radar gun and mount a video camera on the dash. Then I'd drive up and down the interstate and tape all the wacky reactions I inspired in the motorists I tailed or passed.

You know what I mean. Like me, you've probably observed the following types from one lane over or one car back.

First, there are the people we've all seen on the road. They work out their inner rage while driving. In the midst of telling their last four bosses where to get off, they glance into the left lane and realize someone is traveling along parallel to them. Embarrassed, they pretend to be singing along to the radio.

If the car next to theirs is occupied by a trooper, the embarrassment is multiplied tenfold, then gives way to fear: "What if the trooper thinks I'm crazy? Will he pull me over? Will she arrest me?"

Given this scenario, these drivers not only sing along — sometimes to the news and weather — but they also tap the wheel in syncopation, keeping both hands on it, of course.

Next there are the speeders. These people tool along, doing well over the limit, cutting in and out of lanes. But when they glimpse a state police car in their futures, they couldn't slow down any faster if their transmissions dropped out.

The trooper drives past, and they're back on your bumper again.

There are also the people who aren't breaking any law but feel guilty anyway. It's some unresolved childhood thing. They always try to look nonchalant, and succeed only in looking suspicious. This group includes the whistlers.

The funny part is that only innocent people tend to act guilty around police. I'm sure criminals are smooth as silk around them. Maybe that's how police recognize criminals: They're the ones NOT acting guilty.

Many people have told me that they break a sweat when they see a car with one of those light bars coming up on them. But I had a conversation the other day that gave new meaning to the word paranoia.

A woman I work with was telling me how she was driving along Route 9 toward Northampton one day recently, and somewhere around Goshen she noticed that the car directly behind her was occupied by two troopers.

This fact almost caused her to suffer a complete collapse en route.

The problem was that she didn't have her license with her. She knew that because she had lost her license in another city. So she became obsessed with the notion that she might be stopped and found out. This was to be avoided at all costs.

She began following every law to the letter. If the speed limit was 35, she drove exactly 35. She kept her eyes fixed on the road. She was the model motorist.

But wait, she thought then. "What if I'm being TOO careful?" What if they noticed her compulsive behavior and began to suspect she was hiding something? Maybe they'd think she was transporting cocaine for a South American cartel, or had someone tied up and gagged in the trunk.

Oh, irony of ironies. What if by following the laws so precisely, she actually prompted the police to stop her and ask for her license and registration?

The miles seemed to stretch into infinity. She thought about pulling in somewhere, but where? She saw a sign — Bacon's. She didn't know what Bacon's was. How could she stop there? Maybe it was a place where someone like her would have no reason to stop. If she stopped there, the troopers would be on to her for sure.

She drove on. So did they. Finally, in desperation, she pulled in at the Williamsburg Post Office. The troopers continued down Route 9. She was free.

No, wait again. What if they glanced in their rear-view mirror, or doubled back, and saw that she had transacted no business at the post office? Then they'd know she had been trying to escape their surveillance.

She did the obvious. She went in and bought stamps.

Now, THIS is neurotic.

Not that you can ever have too many stamps. But if she had stopped at a funeral home, would she have prepaid her funeral?

At any rate, this woman eluded capture by the Massachusetts State Police. Her license has been returned to her by a Good Samaritan. She has resumed the life of a law-abiding citizen.

So it all turned out fine, except I'll bet those troopers wish they had her on videotape.

They've Got
Some Gall To Ask

When I returned to work recently after having my gall bladder removed, many people said cheerily, "We're expecting a funny column about your operation."

They meant to be friendly, I'm sure, but I was surprised by the expectation. Call me a curmudgeon, but being drugged into insensibility and having my body punctured with ugly instruments is not my idea of a laugh riot. People who think such things are entertaining should tape the gory scenes on "ER" and "Chicago Hope" and play them over and over again, preferably while eating barbecued ribs.

When I have begged off writing the column, however, the response frequently has been a disappointed, "Oh come on, SOMETHING funny must have happened."

It is for these poor sick souls that I offer the following account. If they find it funny, fine.

My operation originally was scheduled for New Year's Eve — well, New Year's Eve day actually. Even I would have balked at having that initial incision made as the champagne corks popped.

I was excited; I liked the idea of keeping with the "out with the old" theme, not to mention having a REALLY big date for New Year's Eve.

But I was stood up. My surgeon opted to postpone and since I could not do it without her, I had to wait.

So on a gray January morning, clad in my ridiculous johnny, seriously pre-shrunk pants and jaunty little cap, I was wheeled into the operating room. I waved a breezy good-bye to my friend while hoping my heart would not explode with sheer terror.

As I lay there shaking hard enough to rattle the gurney, someone fiddled with my IV and said kindly, "OK, you'll start to relax soon."

Relax? That was the understatement of the decade. If I had relaxed any more, I could have been installed in a rock garden.

The surgical team members were free to do with me what they would. (I only hope they exchanged as much witty repartee as the teams do on television because I may have heard it on an unconscious level, and it will make me funnier.)

When I awoke several hours later in a regular hospital room, nurses were standing at my left side and chatting about my blood pressure — or lack of it. It seems I was well below the norm — the down side of being gorked on morphine — and they were discussing what to do about it.

The up side of being gorked on morphine is that I really didn't care what they did. I busied myself with the monumental task of opening my eyes, which seemed to have been Superglued shut. My efforts seemed doomed. I would get one eye cranked open and focused on something only to have the other slam shut.

Eventually, someone told me to just keep them closed. Seemed like a good idea at the time.

I'm told that my first clear sentence was: "I feel like there's a belly sitting on my elephant." But I don't believe it.

Somewhere along the line I had a visitor — a friend of

many years and the veteran of several surgical procedures. You could say she has spent more time lying on a table than your average place setting.

I remember her saying, "Are you in pain?" I must have said yes because she responded, "Take the pain you are feeling and multiply it by 150 times and that's how much pain I had with my first surgery."

I think it was meant to be a pep talk. Boy, talk about tough love.

In the weeks preceding surgery, I had dreamed of hopping off the operating table and whipping up some onion dip, but it was not to be. For the next 36 hours Jell-O was my closest friend.

I thought of the 2,000 doughnuts I had eaten in the six years since I realized that my gall bladder was in revolt. I had known the day of reckoning was getting ever closer. Still, I did not repent until the scalpel had done its work.

With that in mind, and noting the unhappy post-surgical state of my abdomen, I grasped the hand of a friend and delivered this heartfelt advice in measured if raspy tones: "Don't ...eat...fat."

I also recall saying such things as, "I have to be more careful about my diet. I don't want my next operation to be a triple bypass."

As I told my doctor, however, "Without the gall bladder pain as a control, I fear I'll be snorting mayonnaise straight from the jar." Time will tell.

I spent one night in the hospital and three weeks at home. My recovery was punctuated by two icy storms, which I watched from the window while sipping hot tea.

I am back to work now. Sometimes I think of my time spent in the recliner, enjoying the company of Regis and Kathie Lee, while my friends shopped, cooked, carried, shoveled snow and offered floral tributes.

And occasionally I whisper to myself, only to myself: "How bad could a triple bypass be?"

Express Checkout
Provides Food for Thought

Of all the things I hate about grocery shopping, the thing I generally hate most is going through what is laughingly referred to as the express checkout.

People do not seem to understand the governing principle: that this line is meant for shoppers who have purchased only a few items. Bread, milk, dessert for unexpected guests, even, heaven forfend, a pack of cigarettes — these are bona fide express-line items.

That seems simple enough, right? And you'd think the signs that say "12 items or fewer" lighted up like theater marquees would give people a clue.

But there's always got to be that woman trying to slip an extra two — or 20 — items onto the belt: What, is FRUIT considered one item in her house?

And there's often someone who has to step out of line to run back for one more package of Milkbones. That forces the rest of us to stand there wondering if Oprah really fled in tears, and whether we need yet more disposable razors.

Moreover there's seldom a bagger at the express

registers so the cashier has to do double duty, which means the process ends up taking twice as long as it would at the regular checkout. You might as well be behind the family with the three-cart caravan.

Aside from the time I spend waiting in the express line, I have a philosophical objection to its misuse.

I happen to believe that people should shop in an organized, orderly way — once a week perhaps — and take their purchases through the regular checkout.

If they happen to forget or run out of something truly crucial for survival, such as Fig Newtons, they may return to the store to purchase it.

Then, and only then, do they have reason to use the express checkout.

My overall goal here is to minimize time spent in the grocery store, which to my mind is the 10th circle of Dante's inferno.

The other night, however, I had an interesting experience in the express line. What always has been a tedious waste of time in the past became for a few minutes wildly entertaining — if only to me.

I was with a friend, picking up milk and seltzer — both on the approved express-line list.

Standing directly in front of us was a man who looked like a cross between an escaped convict and a long-distance runner: rail thin, nervous, a little unkempt, obviously tired. He seemed to be in a hurry as he shifted from one foot to another and fiddled with the shrink-wrapped package in his hand.

When he placed his single item on the belt, my friend started to smile. A moment later, as the cashier rang it up, I got a glimpse of the package. It looked like ribs — but it wasn't.

"Crab legs," my friend informed me, speaking as softly as she could while giggling like a madwoman.

I'm not quite sure what was so amusing about it. Maybe it was because it was 8 p.m. and it had been a hellacious day and we couldn't imagine anyone actually getting into his car, driving to the store, parking, then standing in line to buy crab legs.

Being out of crab legs isn't like being out of baby formula, you know?

We began to imagine scenarios.

Was there a pot of melted butter sitting on his stove? Did he remember everything for that surf'n'turf buffet except the crab legs?

Was his wife standing at the window, tapping her toe and glancing at the clock, muttering, "Where IS that fool with my crab legs, dammit?"

Or was he a felon trying to break a counterfeit hundred-dollar bill? He had to buy something, so he grabbed a package of crab legs?

Had he been sitting around a poker table with some buddies? Did he suddenly push back his chair and announce, "Hey man, I'm going down to the store for some crab legs. Need anything?"

Do some people get a hankering for crab legs like others get a hankering for pizza?

This was more hilarity that I could stand. But when we managed to make it to the car, still chortling, my friend dropped the bombshell.

She had gotten a closer look and discovered they WEREN'T EVEN REAL CRAB LEGS: they were seafood legs.

Seafood legs? Is the seafood a fish, or a crustacean?

No, she explained, they take a bunch of fish-like stuff and mush it all together. Then they shape it into leg-like projections and voila! Seafood legs.

Oh, I said, pleased that I had learned something during my stint in the express line.

I'm so excited that I may drop by the store tonight to see who's there and what they're buying. I'll pick up some bread while I'm at it. One item — it should only take a minute.

Betty: If You're out There, Call Your Friend

Here's an ethical question: What do you do when there's a message on your answering machine from someone you have never heard of?

Is it OK to ignore and erase the message? Or must you call the party back and tell him or her that the message was left on the wrong machine?

This is not a simple yes-or-no question. There are gray areas — vast gray areas — here.

I had such a message on my machine the other day.

"Hi Betty," the cheerful voice said. It was a woman and she was calling to tell Betty that there was going to be some sort of shindig for those "loyal to the cause."

No kidding. That's what she said: "Loyal to the cause." She wanted Betty to be her guest and would pick her up. She also wanted Betty to call her back, and she left a seven-digit number, which she said was her beeper number.

"I hope your mother is feeling better," she said finally. Then she hung up.

This was not the first message I have received that was clearly not intended for me. Most of the others have been from doctors' offices intending to remind someone of an appointment.

I can see how this can happen. Some poor billing clerk or receptionist who has to make 50 such calls every day dials the wrong number, has no idea what the voice on the machine is supposed to sound like, and delivers the message by rote.

That's understandable.

By the same token, I feel no burning need to inform such a caller of the error. If there's something serious at stake, the office will try the patient again, or the patient will call the office.

In any case, I simply can't solve everybody's problems. I have enough to do trying to run my friends' lives against their will.

Speaking of friends, one of mine had a series of messages wrongly left on her answering machine last year. The man thought he was calling a coworker and kept saying, in tones of increasing urgency: "If you don't come in tomorrow, the boss is going to be really ticked off" — or words to that effect. "Call me," he'd plead at the end of each message.

He didn't leave a number, however, so the boss must have gotten apoplectic and the man's coworker must have gotten canned. Such is life.

Once in a while some breathless teen-ager leaves a message for his girlfriend on my machine. "I love you," he says. "Yeah, I love you too," I say as I press erase.

I think people should be more careful about leaving personal messages on a machine when the voice on the tape is totally unfamiliar to them. Does this kid think his girlfriend has a secretary?

Still, when it came to the call from Betty's friend, I couldn't just brush it off. It sounded to me as if Betty had a rough winter, with her mother being sick. She probably needed a night out. And it wasn't going to cost her anything.

I pondered for a while. Then I dialed the number. Alas!

It was not in the 413 area code. The call had been made from outside western Massachusetts. What was my obligation now?

I had a couple of alternatives available to me. I could have dialed that same number using various area codes. If the woman was willing to pick Betty up, it's safe to assume that she wasn't calling from Nome, Alaska.

But she could have been calling from area codes 617, 508, 203... how far did I have to take this? Did I have to buy a headset and install a second line?

My initial burst of good will did not last long. The more I thought about it, the more rationalizations I came up with.

Loyal to what cause? Maybe Betty was a member of some anarchistic organization and her friend's phone was bugged and by calling that number I would find myself in the middle of a Tom Clancy novel.

What if the cause to which they are loyal is a cause I oppose?

To hell with them both, I decided. I cleared the message.

But now I feel guilty.

So if your name is Betty and your mom has been sick and you have a friend who carries a beeper, this message may be for you.

Your friend wanted to take you somewhere nice, free. I hope that makes you feel better.

If you're loyal to the cause, you know who you are.

I wish I did.

Some Cold Hard Facts
About Job Interviews

There are many markers along the road to curmudgeon-dom, and I'm passing them faster than an Amtrak express. One came into view last week when I read a comment in a news story.

A woman mentioned being asked during a job interview to name her favorite ice-cream flavor.

Now, I know I'm out of step with the times: I don't want a fax machine, for example. But when and how did ice-cream preference become a factor in hirings?

I interviewed for a high-powered corporate job only once, with a manufacturing company in Connecticut. I had decided it would be nice to make a lot of money.

So I played along through the first couple of rounds, spouting what I imagined to be the party line. And since I kept getting sent onward to yet another interviewer I must have been on the right track.

Finally, a snippy woman in a suit that cost more than my car leaned back in her leather chair and said: "So, tell me why you would like to be a part of the XXXXXX family."

I sat there a minute thinking how much I didn't want

to be saying good morning to her for the next five years. Then I smiled and said, "I don't believe I said I did."

The next sound I heard was the door closing behind me. I laughed all the way home.

I guess I don't know why you have to play parlor games to get a job. Whatever happened to questions about what you did in your last position and why you want this one?

Presumably, one's answer to a goofy query gives some insight into his or her personality.

But here's a news flash: The people being asked the questions are trying to give answers they think the people doing the asking want to hear. So the job interviewer might just as well cut the baloney and ask straightforward, germane questions.

Not only does that ice-cream query strike me as inane, but also the asker is fairly begging to be outsmarted — and there are countless ways to do that.

For instance, if applying for a job in which diversity is key, don't say you prefer vanilla. It will make you appear bland, boring — a white-bread person.

Instead, choose a flavor whose name conveys a nice mix: a ripple, maybe, or a swirl.

Don't ever pick strawberry. It's tasty but it's pink and may be associated in the questioner's mind with children's penicillin and/or little girls. It is therefore not a good choice if you want to be regarded as a capable adult.

Rocky Road may convey an impression of toughness, aggressiveness. This is good if you are applying for a job calling for those traits, such as prison guard, but probably wouldn't get you a day-care position.

Heavenly Hash can get you off on the wrong foot with an agnostic or an atheist — no frame of reference. Moreover, anything with "hash" in its name may conjure up pictures of the food or the drug so named. I doubt this can enhance your employment chances. Then again, it depends on what job you're after.

You might want to name a flavor with nuts in it — to show you are a little zany, a risk taker — and someone with good teeth (in case the potential employer is trying to cut dental-plan costs.)

Now, when asked the ice-cream question, someone is bound to throw out the name of a frozen-yogurt flavor. That could qualify as non-responsive, but if the questioner will accept it, fine. My take on it is that frozen yogurt, once an alternative, has become the rule in some places. Choosing it will make you seem to be someone influenced by trends.

I'd recommend that when asked about ice cream, you respond accordingly. Sticking with ice cream shows you are not afraid to appear old-fashioned, i.e., that you are not afraid of what others think of your choices.

It also shows you are not afraid of death by coronary disease, which makes you appear rather daring. I like that in a person and maybe your potential boss will also.

If you really want to stand out in the crowd, name a sherbet. It's a little unusual, yet traditional. The person who prefers sherbet is a true individual.

In any case, you would be wise to name a flavor available from various companies. If you pick a Ben & Jerry's flavor, for example, you may be categorized as a yuppie or, worse, a 60s throwback, while a flavor from a premium line will paint you as a fat-cat elitist.

If you select a flavor from a company with a local presence, it will suggest a commitment to the community and respect for the entrepreneurial spirit — a good choice if you're after a job with the Chamber of Commerce.

Naming a flavor sold by a chain will show you to be a person with the common touch. This would be good in the social services.

The key is to have your answer ready — so you can pretend to be sincere and spontaneous.

As for me, I don't think anyone will ever ask me the ice-cream question. I have a hunch that by the time we got to that point in the interview, we'd both have swallowed quite enough.

Frugality Manufactured out of Whole Cloth

Walking through the supermarket last weekend, I came upon a small display rack that stopped me in my tracks.

Not much of what I see in the supermarket surprises me any more. True, I'm old enough to remember when you went to the market to buy food — period. But over the years, I gradually have adapted to finding flashlights and flea powder and lawn furniture between the soda and the frozen food.

It's kind of neat, actually, being able to pick up a toaster at the same time you pick up the bread. I'm looking forward to the day my store adds a car dealership over by the motor oil.

So when I say this display surprised me, you have to know that I mean it. In fact, there was a store employee stocking shelves in the next aisle and she kept peeking at me worriedly. I think she was trying to decide whether to summon medical assistance or store security because I stood there so long staring at the rack and shaking my head in amazement.

You see, the three-tiered end rack was piled high with plastic bags whose lettering, in bright primary colors, proudly proclaimed the bags' contents.

And the contents were... (drum roll here) RAGS. Yessir, step right up and get your red-hot rags here.

A 20-ounce bag of cloth scraps for only $1.49; Is that a bargain or what?

If I had any doubt that it was a bargain, I had only to look at the diagonal printing at the top left-hand corner of the bag: "25 percent added value."

You may ask: Does that mean the bag contains 25 percent MORE rags or 25 percent BETTER rags? And what would make a bag of rags better — a tuxedo lapel or two tossed in? I don't know. It does sound like a bargain, though.

I picked up a bag and turned it over to view the contents through the clear unlettered side. The rags were mostly a denim-like blue, medium gray and a kind of pinkish, mauve color. They had ragged edges, as one would expect of rags, but otherwise they seemed sadly lacking to me as rags go.

That's because they all appeared to be the same material — think tacky polyester sweatshirt — and the same size. That prompted me to question what the bag promised, namely that the rags were absorbent and good for — make that "ideal" for — "automotive, shop and household uses."

Well, maybe they'd be ideal if you just wanted to dab at a spill or wipe off a dipstick. But if you had a big, disgusting, sloppy mess to clean up, these rags would seem pretty puny.

Besides, I happen to believe that rags should be made, not born. Ragdom is where clothing and linens and towels go when they die. The rag-bag is supposed to contain old T-shirts, undergarments with the elastic missing, towels worn thin, too-small flannel pajamas.

But the secret to success in business, someone once said, is to find a need and fill it, and apparently there is a need for rags. It is a need I do not understand, much like the craving for tofu. But sure enough, someone is out there manufacturing rags and putting them into neat little bags and selling them.

A friend asked me: When a company makes rags, do they start with clothing then tear it up? Or do they make big bolts of cloth then rip them into small pieces and declare the pieces rags?

"That's something to think about," I told her.

I also wondered about the flip side of that issue: If I bought 100 bags of rags and stitched them together, would I have a $149 sweatsuit?

There was another bit of information on the bag worth pondering. The rags are packaged in Canada for a company called Concordia Cloth Inc., which is based, I think, in Massachusetts — there was no town name, just a ZIP code.

Apparently the Bay State business couldn't find anyone in this country to stuff rags into a plastic bag. Or maybe Corcordia was aiming at snob appeal— offering rags imported from Canada, like bottled water.

This rag business strikes me as more evidence that we have lost the knack for frugality. We think using Ziploc bags or tinfoil more than once qualifies us for an ecology award, when in other times, people relied on plain waxed paper.

I asked someone from a big family how she thought this buying and selling of prepackaged rags came about. She said, "It's because people don't wear their clothes out anymore." She paused, then added, "They give them to me."

Maybe so. But at some point in the process, garments have to end up somewhere. Where will that be if people are making their rags from scratch?

Who knows? Anyway, if you need rags, and you honestly can't find an old nightgown in your house, you can go to my supermarket and look for them in the vicinity of the wastebaskets and disposable diapers.

Now, if you should happen to need dust — any kind, any amount — call me. Have I got a deal for you.

Sprain Causes Pain — Little of It in the Knee

A few weeks ago I sprained my left knee. It hurt a lot for a short time and probably will hurt a little for a long time, as knee injuries do.

But I found the physical injury less troublesome than: 1. explaining it, and 2. answering a surveyor's questions about the medical care I received.

First of all, there is no point in recounting a boring minor injury, so you might as well just ignore people when they ask what happened.

If you sprain something while sinking a three-point basket in the last 30 seconds of a championship game, or sprinting across the finish line in the Ironman Triathlon, or saving someone from certain death, that might be moderately interesting to people.

But I hurt myself while engaged in the arduous activity of getting up from a chair and taking a step.

It could have been much worse. I could have fallen, for example. But I was able to keep myself upright, thanks to years of practice and an intense conditioning regimen that includes getting up from a variety of chairs many, many times each day whether I need to or not.

Sometimes I virtually catapult myself out of a recliner. This requires me to pull a lever with my right hand, simultaneously kick down the footrest and spring to a standing position in one fluid motion.

Some who have seen me do this tell me it's poetry in motion. You've heard of Air Jordan. Meet Chair Robbins. But such feats lose much in the telling.

So, given that the story of this mishap is a snoozer, I made up some different accounts. I told some people an old war injury had flared up, others that I'd been wounded. It didn't matter. Most people don't pay much attention anyway. They only ask to be nice. So I muttered something in each case and they all seemed pleased with themselves for inquiring.

The days passed slowly, though they moved faster than I did on crutches, and all was well — until the Grand Inquisitor called me.

He introduced himself as someone conducting a market survey for the hospital I went to for assistance.

He wanted to inquire about my experience at said hospital, he said, adding, "Would this be a good time to talk briefly?"

If it really would be brief, I said.

Oh yes indeedy it would, he assured me.

I was anxious that the call not be lengthy because a friend had driven in from the Sturbridge area to pick up groceries for me, and I believe anyone who delivers food to my door deserves my undivided attention.

But I also sympathize with people who make their living calling other people who don't want to be called, so I tried to be cheerful.

We went through basic information and about 10 seconds into the conversation I stated clearly that I had only been at the hospital for about two hours total, and that I had sprained a knee.

This guy apparently was on automatic pilot, because none of that made a difference to him as he asked his 1,012 questions — well, it seemed like that many.

Had I seen the hospital chaplain? he asked. Did I like the food? Did I feel that the necessary equipment had been available?

"This wasn't open-heart surgery," I snapped in response to the last one. "It was a sprain."

He was dauntless. I don't know if people in the past have slammed down the phone on him or what, but he charged through that list like a man on a mission.

My favorite question: At any point was I denied assistance in bathing?

I was glad he gave me a chance to vent my feelings on that one, because interestingly enough, while lying there waiting to be seen by the doctor, I did have a sudden urge to shower and there was just no one around to help. They all must have been frittering away their time and energy on someone with a gaping wound or something.

Other questions ranged from how attentive the nurses were to how comfortable the temperature was.

Contributing to the endlessness of this was the fact that I couldn't just say yes or no or fine or good. Everything was on a scale.

For example, a query such as "were the technicians friendly?" might be answered by: not friendly at all, somewhat friendly, ordinarily friendly, very friendly, or so friendly you need a restraining order.

Get the idea? I'm telling you that women have been in labor less time that I was on the phone.

Finally, it was over. I was exhausted.

Then he told me I might get a call from his supervisor asking about him — "how professional I was."

Actually he was between very professional and extremely professional. But not flexible at all.

Unearthing New Talents
in Her Own Backyard

It seems that every time you think you have people pegged, they surprise you.

Take this friend of mine, for example. Based on all my past interaction with her, I thought I had her figured.

If you had asked me to describe her, I would have said she is a bookstore sort of person: someone who cares about the fabric content of her clothes; a thoughtful, reflective type who actually reads The New York Times.

Now I discover that she indeed may be all those things but she has taken on a whole new dimension, one that concerns me almost as much as it confuses her.

She has acquired a house, complete with a yard. And she is getting into it in a big way.

I knew this purchase would change her, but I imagined she would take on the role of the landed gentry — sitting under a shade tree reading poetry and sipping iced tea with mint as the "yard man" tended to the flower beds.

But oh no. She has begun to put down her book and pick up a spade. She has traded her pen for a hoe.

In short, she has turned into a lover of the land, a tiller of the soil — she has taken up gardening.

Now, if I had seen this coming, I might have been able to intercede in time. But it's too late now. The mania for growing things has taken hold.

Personally, I think people are born with or without the gardening gene. But even if you want to stretch the point and presume that a green thumb can be developed, the way a guitar player develops a callus, there should be an age cutoff.

Certainly, it would be best to start this gardening business at your mother's , or father's, knee. But even if you take it up in your 20s, it's OK. Your expertise and confidence will grow with your petunias, and you're still young enough to memorize the names of flowers.

But when you begin gardening in your 30s, or later, you bring to it many problems: bad joints; a morbid fear of things that creep, crawl and dive-bomb you; and, worst of all, the paralyzing insecurity that most adults have about trying new things.

That's been the hardest part for my friend.

This is new ground for her, so to speak, and she has doubts about her prowess.

People who can diagram a sentence and spell words like "ubiquitous" without looking them up sometimes have a difficult time making the transition from reading *The Good Earth* to digging in it.

I have long known, but am reminded by her experience, that a neophyte or inexpert gardener should work only in the back of the house, or by the light of the moon.

It's too embarrassing otherwise.

I have gone outside with my pruning shears and nipped at a bush tentatively, almost shyly, certain that the man across the street is rolling around on his sunporch, guffawing. "Look at that fool across the street," I imagine him telling his wife. "Does she expect that bush to live?"

On some intellectual level, I know this man is too busy

dragging his hedge-clippers around his own yard to worry about mine. But this has nothing to do with intellect.

So, if my bush should die before that man does, I will have no choice but to steal away while he is sleeping and begin a new life somewhere else — in an apartment.

My friend's recent experience has reminded me of all my own neuroses along this line.

Out in her yard not long ago, armed with shiny new implements, she stood befuddled. She had dug the hole. The bush awaited. Now what? Was the hole deep enough? Was it too deep? Should she just drop the bush in, or what?

At that moment, a stranger ambled up the street.

Obviously, she didn't want him to see what she was doing. She was afraid he would come plodding up the drive to say, "Excuse me, madam. I know I'm a complete stranger but I must tell you: Only an idiot would put that bush there."

So what did she do?

"I went back into the house," she confessed.

Yes, it is pathetic by most standards. But I think she did very well.

I would have put all the dirt back in the hole.

A Garnish or
Two Can't Hurt

Most newspapers have a policy of publishing weekly lunch menus for schools — and senior-citizen meal sites — as a service. Over the years I have perused more than my share of them.

I have found the offerings very similar from week to week — and from place to place. You might even say these menus are a trifle boring. I find myself hoping the food is more interesting to eat than it is to read about.

Try it for yourself. Skim a whole week's listing and familiar phrases will keep popping out: chicken nuggets, hot dogs, "tater tots," potato sticks, garden salad, choice of dressing.

There are the tried-and-true, stick-to-the-ribs entrees such as macaroni and cheese and hot turkey sandwich with gravy. And there's something called "school-baked chicken" — not to be confused with chicken baked elsewhere and trucked in, I guess.

A few more exotic offerings might catch your eye: ravioli, kielbasa, pork sausage pattie, and "lazy lasagna," which I picture as lasagna in which the cheese is too lethargic to melt.

My favorite item to date is the ever popular "blue gelatin with topping." Good blue food is hard to find.

Whether you love or hate such foods, someone should pep up the descriptions of them in the paper, which are lacking a certain panache.

And I think I know just the people who could do it: the folks who write the menus for some area restaurants. I'm referring to the menus that describe the most mundane dish as a culinary fantasy, making a simple hamburger sound like something Julia Child would serve to outdo Martha Stewart.

In many cases, these menu writers could qualify for the Pulitzer prize for fiction: The meal served bears no resemblance to the fabulous description provided.

But even then, I bow to them. They have the gene shared by every food writer — in whose presence all edible things become flaky, tangy, creamy, crunchy, crispy, golden brown or piquant.

Sometimes the muse gets out of hand — for the person concocting the dish, the person writing about it, or both. One former Northampton restaurant in particular always had in every offering about two ingredients too many for my taste.

For example, the description of a tuna sandwich on most menus might read: "solid white tuna mixed with chopped onion and celery and served on blah, blah, blah.

But at that particular restaurant, the onion had to be a red onion — make that a sweet red onion — and the chef just had to add pesto mayonnaise, or a dollop of goat cheese, or three chopped artichoke hearts, two roasted red peppers and a goose egg on a spit.

Lots of restaurants do that to some degree. Apparently, they believe people won't order — or enjoy — an ordinary sandwich or omelet or salad. There has to be an element of surprise involved. "Oh wow, they put radicchio on my ham and cheese."

"You think that's something? This sliced kiwi really perks up my peanut butter and jelly."

Chances are the food on the school lunch line, or the senior citizen's tray, won't change much, given budgets, special dietary requirements and the need to please a lot of different palates.

But if the people creating the fancy restaurant menus could get ahold of the school and senior lunch listings, at least the menus would be a lot more exciting.

Below is an example of an actual school lunch as described in the Gazette listing, and the description as it would read if "tweaked" by a creative menu writer.

ACTUAL SCHOOL LUNCH: Roll, chicken nuggets, potato puffs, cucumber slices, macaroni salad.

ENHANCED VERSION: Four-grain roll topped with sesame seeds; chicken tidbits breaded in cornmeal and fried in canola oil till crusty; crispy potato morsels; thin slices of English cucumber marinated in balsamic vinegar and pure olive oil and highlighted with a hint of basil; tricolor pasta tossed in a light mayonnaise and peppercorn dressing and served on a bed of arugula.

It's like poetry, isn't it? I'm telling you, if they wrote it up this way in the newspaper, the kitchens wouldn't be able to keep up with the demand. The food would fairly fly out of the pots and onto the plates.

In one category, of course, there would be little change. What the school lunch menu refers to as "manager's choice" becomes the "chef's special" in the restaurant version.

In my house, I call that dish "cleaning out the refrigerator."

Not Easy to Remember, But So Hard to Forget

Remember when you were in school and some teacher told you that your brain could hold way more data than you could ever possibly put into it?

I had my doubts about that then. Now I don't believe it for a minute. Clearly, the teacher who told me that had no vision of a future with innumerable cable television channels, area codes and nine-digit ZIP codes to remember.

That's why I was fascinated the other night when an old friend explained to me her theory of memory. It was one I could so readily accept.

"It's a filing system," she said. "If the W's are full and you need to file something under W, you need to throw something out to make room for it."

There's always plenty of room in the Z's and Q's, she noted. But the vowels? You're constantly clearing out the vowels, she said.

That's why you can't remember anyone in your seventh-grade social-studies class whose name began with A. It's hopeless. Don't even try.

Obviously, there are serious memory deficits caused by accident or illness. That is not what we are talking about here. We are talking about those memory lapses that have been blamed — unfairly it seems to me — on "normal aging."

It is true that the mere passage of time is at the root of the problem, but not because time dims our mental powers. No, rather it is because time triggers the automatic expiration dates built into our mental filing system.

There were no microchips when the human brain was invented, no diskettes. If our brains are computers, they are computers with a hard drive, which must store everything, forever — and obviously cannot.

At newspapers, we put a "kill date" on every story. On that date, the story will "fall out" of the system, disappear, go to cyber heaven. Sometimes they ask us to manually purge our files before the kill dates take effect because the system is getting overloaded.

When it gets overloaded, it slows down and is unwilling to accept new data.

See the parallel?

Certainly, we have an automatic kill system in our brains. We are constantly dumping files that have not been accessed in, say, more than 20 years. (I'm not sure of the timing. This is not my theory, after all. Maybe my friend told me. I don't remember.)

So if you are over age 40 and run into someone at K mart who was in ninth grade with you and you can't remember his name, it's no big deal. Who cares anyway? If he mattered to you, you'd have thought of him once in a while. You haven't, and he dropped out of your file. So what? He doesn't remember your name either.

Smile and move on. You have more important things to think about, like where you left your car.

If you remember things you stuffed into your brain even 50 or 60 years ago, it is because you keep calling them up on your mental screen. That is why one person can immediately access a recipe for banana bread — no cookbook required — while another can dash off the chemical symbol for nitrogen. The latter fact is one I purged so quickly and efficiently from my mind in high school that I was urged to remove myself from the chemistry class. The day I did so was a day of much rejoicing and will live in my memory — and the teacher's — forever.

The point is that if it is important to you to remember someone or something, you need only think about them periodically to keep the file active. Otherwise, forget about them altogether. Clear the decks. Make room for some more meaningful or useful information.

Now, if you want to dump some files, how do you do it? Well, you can let them drop out automatically, of course. But what if you can't wait; you need to make room now? There's a technique that may help.

Say that you wrote a paper on Chaucer's *Canterbury Tales* when you were in college. Unless you teach Chaucer, it's a safe bet that the pardoner, the nun, and the rest of the gang will never come up in your daily conversation.

So call them up on your mental screen, say: "Who needs it?" and never think of it again.

To put this in its simplest terms: The key to remembering more is to think about less, less often.

That's why when people accuse me of engaging in mindless pursuits — when I watch 20 consecutive hours of television, for example — I say, "Hey do you mind? I'm working on improving my memory here. And don't you forget it."

As You Sow - or Don't - So Shall You Reap

A friend confided to me recently that her sister-in-law is in a terrible predicament. I feel it cries out to be shared — because not many people could get themselves into, let alone out of, this particular mess.

The sister-in-law lives in a small New Hampshire town. A teacher by profession, she is not working right now. So she is "involved in the community," as they say.

One form that involvement has taken is membership in the garden club. So happy was the club to have her as a member, that she was elected vice president soon after joining. Or maybe they couldn't find anyone else willing to be vice president.

In either case, she has the title. Nice, huh?

It seems the club members take turns meeting at each other's homes. This is a folksy New England-type tradition. It is helpful, too, because most garden clubs can't afford to build meeting halls.

I'm writing this in June. In July, it will be the sister-in-law's turn to act as host of the meeting in her very own home. This is why she's in distress.

It's not that she doesn't like to entertain. She can slap together a few sandwiches, put on a pot of coffee. She has plates that match.

It's the agenda that worries her. The members expect to chat about whatever garden enthusiasts like to chat about, partake of a little refreshment, then tour her garden.

Oops, we're in trouble now.

She doesn't have a garden.

That's right. You got it. She is vice president of the garden club and she has no garden.

"It just happened," my friend told me.

How? I asked. First of all, why does someone join a garden club if she has no garden? Did she envision a grand garden and grow weary in the planning stages?

"She likes to garden. She used to have a garden," my friend explained. "But she hasn't had one for a couple of years."

She amended that: She does have asparagus and rhubarb — mundane stuff — but none of those exquisite perennials that garden clubbers would be apt to get excited about.

"She has garden space, but it's filled with weeds," my friend added.

The sister-in-law must find a way out of this bind.

This isn't a geometry final: She can't just come down with a cold and buy herself another day or two. She'll have to have the gang over, all right. And she'll have to stand there and meet their questioning gazes when they look at a plot filled with weeds.

Instead of "how does your garden grow?" they'll be asking "where did your garden go?"

This isn't a federal offense. There's really no requirement that you have a garden when you join a garden club, I suppose, but I think most people would assume you had one. Or, that you would have mentioned NOT having one. This is bound to be embarrassing.

So, what to do?

I offered two suggestions. The first: that she hire a landscaper and pay whatever it costs to fake a garden. Just lay in about 300 flats and throw a little dirt over the whole array to cover the sides of the containers.

It could work.

My second idea was more creative — and cheaper.

Have her buy a few plants in bloom — whatever she likes. She won't need a green thumb, because these flowers don't have to last long.

She can go out in the yard at midnight with a spade and knock the stuffing out of the garden space. Dig it up, toss a few cans and bottles around and then scatter the flowers she just bought.

When the club members show up at the door, she can look stunned and shaken and say: "Some MONSTER just vandalized my beautiful garden."

Not only will it get her completely off the hook, but odds are that the club members will feel so sorry for her that they'll bring over plants and flowers by the trunkful and put them in for her — "replacing" her garden.

Of course it's a tad dishonest. So? Let's be realistic. Ever hear of situational ethics?

It's foolproof, I tell you. But I think she'll be too honest to try it. She'll probably fess up, try to make a joke of it and be considered a little zany for the rest of her life. If she hopes to regain any credibility after this, she and her family may have to move.

Meanwhile, my friend tells me this same sister-in-law just became a library trustee.

Oh sure, I said. Can she read?

Cat and Mouse Game: Any Number Can Play

The woman hates mice. It's an irrational hatred, of course, but it goes bone-deep.

Actually she hates all rodents, describing them all in relationship to rats. Squirrels are "just rats with bushy tails," for example. Bunny rabbits are fluffy rats with big ears. Mice are mini rats. (Not baby rats, mind you. She's not an idiot; she knows one animal from another.)

Basically, they're all the same, she'll tell you. They all have those beady little eyes and that jerky scurrying motion. "Yuk," she says when she sees them. Of people who make pets of them — or of hamsters or gerbils or other rat-like critters — she has only this to say: Why?

Let me put it this way: If she had a choice between finding a mouse in the kitchen or wrestling a testy pit bull in the parlor, she'd be putting on her wrestling togs.

So when the cat suddenly froze in front of the hall bookcase one night this summer, it is not surprising that the woman broke into a sweat.

A friend was visiting at the time, and when the woman said, "There's a mouse in the house," the friend scoffed.

"Naw, he's just playing," she said of the cat.

"That is not playing," the woman replied. "That is stalking. That is a highly motivated cat. That is a cat on the job."

Minutes later, as the cat could be heard racing through the house and careening around corners like a Porsche doing 90 mph on Route 141, the friend reassessed the situation. She sighed. "Oh boy," she said.

Then, being a loyal friend, she added, "Well, if he catches it, I'll deal with it."

To the woman, dealing with it meant loading an assault weapon, but she decided to leave the matter to her friend.

They began watching a television program, but the woman was restless. Suddenly, her peripheral vision kicked in — not a moment too soon. The cat was coming toward her with a jaunty step and something clenched between his teeth. Since he is not a pipe smoker, this was cause for alarm.

Like any mature adult under stress, the woman pulled an afghan over her head and drew her knees up to her chest. She probably would still be in that position had the friend not leaped up, true to her word, and taken charge.

After a brief dance routine including several pirouettes and some nice footwork on the staircase, she coaxed the cat to take his prize into the bathroom. Then she slammed the door. The strategy: Let the best quadruped win.

The two women went back to watching the TV program, each pretending not to hear the thuds and scuffles coming from the bathroom. It was like listening to the adventures of Tweety and Sylvester on the radio.

When silence finally descended, they waited another two hours. Then the friend gingerly opened the door.

The cat meowed appreciatively and exited.

The friend steeled herself to deal with the carnage.

But no. There was the mouse sitting in the bathtub. There was no water in the tub, of course; he wasn't soaking in the tub. He was just sitting in it.

"What should I do with him?" the friend asked. "Put him outside?"

"Hell no," the woman shouted. "He'll only come back in."

"Well I can't kill him," the friend wailed.

They pondered. Then the friend made a decision. She scooped the mouse up into a bag and carried it out to her car. The woman watched as they drove off. Talk about your odd couple.

The mouse made no attempt to escape, the friend reported later. He just sat there on the passenger seat.

The friend took him to a shopping center for reasons that remain unclear. It may have been because she likes shopping so much herself that she thought he would enjoy it. Or maybe she figured that where there is food, there is apt to be a large rodent community.

In any case, she put the bag down on a grassy traffic island and the mouse stepped out. "OK, I'm leaving now," the friend said, walking away. When she turned back, the mouse was gone.

This happened several weeks ago. The woman still levitates every time the cat so much as twitches. She remains convinced the mouse is wending his way back to her house.

"Why wouldn't he?" she asks rhetorically of anyone who will listen. It's the "land of the free" for mice: The cats don't kill them and the humans merely resettle them.

For her part, the friend is quite pleased with herself for coming up with the mouse relocation project. She's also awfully glad that it wasn't a squirrel the cat cornered.

It would have been tough to climb an oak tree while holding that bag.

One Person's News, Another Person's Nausea

I figure I should be able to open my medical practice sometime this fall. I think I'll be ready because I've been watching a lot of television, and students at Harvard Medical School probably have seen fewer clinical procedures this month than I have.

One morning I was eating my oatmeal and watching the early news, when I found myself staring at someone's vocal cords — in motion.

I wonder if the average person really needs to see anybody else's vocal cords — especially at 5:30 a.m. I know I don't.

You'd think I would be used to this stuff by now. Since the TV moguls decided a few years ago that the public has an insatiable appetite for medical information, I've seen more beating hearts than a thoracic surgeon.

Local stations and the major networks crank out an endless supply of segments on research breakthroughs, experimental procedures and medical "miracles."

That's all supplemented by the spate of reality-based shows, such as "Rescue 911" reruns, which can hardly make their way through an episode without somebody cutting an umbilical cord in the back of a pickup traveling at high speed.

Actually, I like the reality shows. They are emotionally satisfying — in a manipulative sort of way. When the EMTs finally stop that bungee jumper from ricocheting off the bridge, it melts my stony heart.

On the other hand, I find that medical news on TV is seldom satisfying. In fact, I often find it annoying.

Sometimes it's the information that irritates me. Other times it's the person delivering it.

I don't mind the local reporters doing their standups in front of their friendly neighborhood hospital. Those poor slugs, like most journalists, are just following some editor's orders. I have no bone to pick with them.

Nor am I putting down the community doctors who do TV spots. Some of them actually are pretty good on camera, although you occasionally find one who gazes into the lens like a cat tracking a bird on the opposite side of a window.

The ones who get on my nerves are the physicians hired by the networks, presumably to give medical news more credibility. Maybe they do. I know they give me a sharp, recurring pain.

First off, this full-time TV gig strikes me as a pretty cushy job for a bona fide physician.

Granted anyone who has completed a long, tedious education costing a truckload of money is entitled to parlay a medical degree into a profit. But these doctors hardly seem like doctors. They don't even have to wash their hands — unless they're having dinner with a network VP.

All they really have to do is get good haircuts and solemnly intone such breathtaking pronouncement as: "Americans should eat more bran."

That brings us to the subject matter itself; it seems to tend towards one extreme or the other. Either the topic is so bland and overdone that it gives you narcolepsy, or so high tech and intense that it gives you nightmares.

On the boring end of the spectrum — that's spectrum, not speculum — we get groundbreakers along the lines of "Pork chop fat is not an entree," or "Don't sit in the poison oak."

At the other end are the "Come with us while we actually make an incision" stories — the ones that whisk us into the laboratory, treatment room or surgical suite, where we may get a glimpse of anything from the birth of twins to the removal of ear wax.

Included in this category of not-to-be-missed mealtime entertainment — besides the vocal-cord expose mentioned above — are some of my other personal favorites: cataract removal, liver transplantation and liposuction.

And for a lighter touch, there are always those zany laboratory mice.

I think when a TV station gets its license from the FCC, it is issued the minute of file footage that shows 10 lab mice cavorting in a cage. The station then can show that video any time it has a medical story — along with the tape of that slide viewed through a microscope.

When TV first started providing up-close and personal glimpses of people's innards, I would scream at the set: "If I wanted to spend my life in an operating room, I'd wear a scrub suit, you ghouls."

But I've given up on that. Now I just keep eating my oatmeal.

Someone reading this is bound to ask why I don't change the channel when such footage comes on.

I would. But there's so much of it that if I kept switching stations to escape it, I'd get vertigo.

Besides, since I'm not a board-certified surgeon, it may take me a minute to realize that the unusual landscape on the screen is actually someone's gall bladder, OK?

And by that time, we've moved on to weather and sports.

Say Hello to Jolly
Mr. Sun, Then Run

One of my co-workers came in Monday looking like the cover illustration for the novel *The Masque of the Red Death*. She had been playing tennis without wearing sunscreen. I didn't hesitate to express my opinion of this folly. I think my opening remark to her was something along the lines of, "What are you, nuts?"

Even before serious health risks became associated with too much exposure to the sun, I had my own concerns about it. Now these concerns have been fueled by the objective evidence.

So I berated the poor soul and then, after she admitted she had been a fool and pledged to carry sunscreen in her tennis bag for the rest of her life, I took pity on her.

"Does it hurt?" I asked. She crinkled up her face. "It hurts when I do this."

(Five second pause here).

"So I don't do this."

And I thought vaudeville was dead.

After more such knee-slapping repartee, we began a

brief discussion of how being sun-sensitive can put a crimp in your summer fun.

What it boils down to — excuse the choice of verbs — is that to some people the phrase "sunny summer days" conjures up balmy breezes, picnics in the park, the pounding of the surf, the crack of a bat connecting with a ball.

But to others, sunny summer days are simply the days when jolly Mr. Sun wraps his arms around you and squeezes until you gasp for air and cry out for shade. Then, when you have collapsed, he sends down his toasty warm rays to fry you senseless.

In short, some people like to baste — sorry, bask — in the sun's rays, and others don't. It's all in your point of view, I guess. Or maybe it's partly in your point of view and partly in your skin and body composition.

It seems reasonable to conclude that everyone should be cautious when going out in the sun, and some should be more cautious than others.

My red-faced co-worker, for example, happens to be fair-skinned. That would seem to dictate extra care, i.e., she should know better. And she does.

In fact, she recalled that when she was a small child, her parents used to take the family to Cape Cod every year. The object of such trips usually is to let the children cavort merrily amid the sand and surf. Not in her case.

"My parents would chain me to the umbrella," she said.

I think she was speaking figuratively, but who knows? Maybe she really was shackled to one of those brightly striped umbrellas. Maybe she lay there hour after hour, guzzling Kool-Aid, looking longingly at the water, occasionally reaching out to touch the area just beyond the shade.

A poignant picture? Yeah, so what? It was for her own good. And if her mother had seen her sunburned face the other day, she would have broken out the umbrella and the handcuffs.

I had my consciousness raised on this issue by a couple of bad bouts with the sun during my own childhood.

I remember my back and the skin behind my knees being the shade of ripe watermelon — the inside, not the outside. I remember walking like the Tin Man in *The Wizard of Oz*. Most of all, I remember PAIN.

Nowadays, I'm smart enough not to go out in the sun without taking precautions.

Actually, I try not to go out in the sun at all. Some would suggest that is because I prefer to sit indoors, read trashy novels and sip cool drinks.

But in fact it's because I find the sun sickening. This is not an expression of opinion; it is a statement of fact. Too much sun literally makes me sick. For me the sun does not work like an oven; it works like a microwave: more than two minutes and I'm ruined.

Therefore, when I do sally forth into the great outdoors, I have to take steps to protect myself from the sun. In the past, I have taken measures some might consider extreme. You have to remember that sunscreen, sunblock, whatever you call it, is newer on the scene than I am.

So some years ago, the one and only time I took an island vacation, I was easy to spot.

I was the one trudging along the beach while wearing jeans, a long-sleeved workshirt, sunglasses and a hat. Other, bikini-clad, vacationers probably thought I was in the Witness Protection Program.

I didn't care what they thought, and if I ever had to spend a long period on the beach again, I would opt for the same attire.

It's better than suffering from blisters and sun-poisoning.

And it beats being chained to the umbrella.

Serial Fillers:
Eating Right To Get Thin

There are only a few legitimate ways left to get rich fast in America. You can be a major-league athlete or an outstanding entertainer, win a state lottery — or devise a new diet.

Since I lack coordination, talent and luck, the first three options appear closed to me. Therefore, I've decided to offer the world yet another diet: "The Pam Robbins Quick Weight-Loss System." (A system is more impressive — and expensive — than a diet.)

I think this is a natural progression, since my "Pam Robbins Quick Weight-Gain Diet" has proved itself a huge success.

A mere flip of the nutritional coin and I could be on Easy Street, living in a mansion — maybe even driving a car with decent shocks.

There are two keys to most weight-loss programs: diet and exercise. Mine is different. Those who wish to incorporate exercise certainly may do so, but it is not necessary. The way I see it: If we were meant to spend more time on our feet than on our seats, why would our seats be so much larger?

My program focuses on eating — not what you eat but how you eat it. Intrigued? Wait till the infomercial.

Never mind counting calories or fat grams. Forget the centers and workshops and weekly weigh-ins. Forget the famous and near-famous spokespeople. Forget Harry Belafonte's daughter in particular. What's her name? The one who's made a career out of losing the same eight pounds but keeps changing her hair color to confuse us. Well, forget her.

Forget Susan Powter too. She's the one with no hair and a big voice. She wants to Stop the Insanity — except her own, which is quite lucrative for her.

Actually her diet program is very sensible. But so what? If people wanted to lose weight sensibly, they'd stop eating Big Macs as an appetizer. They want an easy program, a new program, a happening kind of program.

My program is all those things. And while you may never actually lose weight on it, it will keep you entertained until the next one comes along.

Now for the particulars. My program is based on the natural way to eat; the way you ate until your parents interfered.

Remember when you were little? You ate all of your peas, then all of your potatoes, then all of your pot roast.

It worked for you. But would they leave you alone? No. You had to eat a little of this, then a little of that, they said. You probably grew up actually combining foods in the same forkful. Argh!

No wonder our bodies get confused. No wonder we get fat.

Sounds great, huh? I made it up but I can get some cockamamie expert to agree with me. You can find an expert to agree with you about anything if you look hard enough.

Let's see, what else do I need? Photos, testimonials and, since you can't sell ideas, a product or two.

It would be nice to get a celebrity to speak for my plan. But they all seem too busy these days, pushing other diets or hawking their exercise videos.

I don't know any real celebrities anyway. The most famous people I know write for the same paper I do. I guess I'll just stick with testimonials from ordinary folk — the kind I can make up.

The before-and-after photos and testimonials will be packaged together. There will be a blurry snapshot of an unrecognizable woman juxtaposed with a much better photo of a much thinner woman. The two will bear no real resemblance to one another, except for similar hair and really ugly clothing.

The text will say: *Pearl G. of Wyoming* — she ought to be easy to track down, huh? — *says: "This diet worked for me. I was never hungry and now I have more energy than ever before. My husband loves the new me, which is great because he hated the old me. He's so impressed with the Pam Robbins Quick Weight-Loss System that he's started eating all his roast pig before he tackles his side of beef. Thanks, Pam Robbins!"*

As for the product, here it comes. Hold on to your hats. A sectioned plate. Neat, huh? Like the ones they use for babies, with sections for three foods.

No beans sliding into the hot dogs on my diet. No sirree. One food at a time — the way we were meant to eat. Hey, if we were supposed to eat everything at once, apples and oranges would grow on the same tree.

It makes no sense, you say? Does drinking your meals make sense?

I'm telling you, this can sell.

So anyone interested in helping me with start-up costs can call me. We'll get together over breakfast. I say we eat the doughnuts first.

More Things
Are Lost Than Found

To the person who has my sweater: All right, I'm ready to negotiate. Unmarked bills in a brown paper bag? What denominations? The Coolidge Bridge at dawn? OK, I'll come alone — whatever. Let's talk. PAM.

Sorry to use this column to place a personal ad of sorts, but I'm desperate. My sweater has been missing for weeks now, and I HAVE TO have it back.

It's an old sweater, but my mom gave it to me and I was attached to it. Not only do I miss it, but frankly, its continued absence is having a detrimental effect on my mental state.

I've begun to show signs of agitation, irritability and paranoia. I'm feeling unkindly toward my fellow humanoids.

How is this different from my previous state? I guess it's a matter of degree.

The sweater had been draped over the back of my office chair for about eight years. I enjoyed having it here. I especially liked the way it would slip down and bunch up behind me, and the way I could roll my chair over at least one of the sleeves a couple hundred times a day. It gave me a good excuse to jump up, utter an expletive, rearrange the sweater and sit back down. Very sound behavior, ergonomically speaking.

My sweater was one of those familiar things that breed a false sense of security. You think they will always be there. Then, in an instant, they are gone, and you realize how fond of them you had become.

When the sweater was not on my chair that first Monday morning, people said, "Oh, it will turn up." I wanted to, tried to, believe them.

I kept an eye open, posted a memo, passed the word. I pleaded, cajoled, threatened bodily harm. The quest took on a life of its own, as quests usually do. (Really, what would they have DONE with the Holy Grail?)

I've flirted with the notion of a conspiracy: Someone took it on purpose just to drive me nuts. I've considered the stranger-in-the-building theory. I've wondered if some passing teen-ager took my sweater for a kind of joy ride and then abandoned it somewhere, torn and with a couple of buttons missing.

Most of my colleagues took a less strident tack. "Someone probably borrowed it and forgot to return it," one murmured reassuringly. All around me, heads nodded.

"Oh, sure," I thought. "It's easy to forget that you're wearing a 12-pound cable-knit sweater THAT ISN'T YOURS." (All right. I didn't just think that; I said it — more than once.)

Fact is: This sweater is so bulky it could have kept Admiral Perry warm. It defies folding. It won't easily fit in a drawer. It's hard to miss.

I've concluded that if the sweater wasn't taken deliberately, then it has gone to join my class rings on some plane we cannot see but must believe exists.

Within a few years of my college graduation, I lost one ring, replaced it, lost the second, and bought a third. Fortunately, the third one is too small, so I never wear it. This virtually guarantees it won't be lost.

I feel triumphant. I have defeated the forces that govern the disappearance of rings. If I remain ringless, it is only because of too many doughnuts, which themselves are rings. You see the symmetry of it?

Yet, even all these years later, I still look for those rings. If we move a piece of furniture, or empty out a storage box, I hope to catch a glint of metal. When we had a furnace replaced a while back, I was downstairs poking around in the debris, sure that at least one of those rings — tourmaline in a gold setting — had slipped through a large heating vent in the floor, along with assorted coins, ballpoint pens and teaspoons. No luck. If they were there, the scrap-metal dealer is wearing them now.

Similarly, I'm still looking for the sweater, still hoping — expecting even — to find it in a bathroom, or under a desk or hanging from a coatrack.

I have not ruled out a reward for information leading to its return. I'm willing to accept the phone charges from any out-of-town informants out there. I'll take a meeting anytime, dispatch an emissary anywhere.

In a word, I would gladly take it back, no questions asked.

But just as I never found the rings, I'll most likely never regain the sweater. Life can be a frustrating affair. Best to surrender in these cases and move on.

And I will. But first I'd like to mention that it's an off-white sweater with a shawl collar and pockets. Keep an eye out for it, will you? Oh, and for two rings, both tourmalines.

The Great Sweater
Mystery Unraveled

The letter was printed on white blue-lined paper and folded twice. I glanced at the signature first. It was signed "Oatsie (not my real name.)" Then I began reading.

"Here's your stupid sweater bak," it said. "When I seen the article in the paper, I thought I better return it."

It went on for several paragraphs, replete with errors in spelling and verb forms — all inserted in a clever attempt to disguise the identity of the writer — a devout and practicing grammarian.

Fact is, I already knew who wrote it. She had confessed the night before on the phone.

I knew when I heard her voice that something was up. Though we work together, we only phone each other during national emergencies or when something really, really major happens at work.

For instance, if a man and woman have lunch together more than once in the same week, one of us might call the other to decide whether the two make a suitable couple or not.

So she had my attention when she began: "Pam, tell me about the buttons on your sweater."

Hmmn, I thought, she's losing it. She's calling me to talk about my missing sweater, a matter not nearly weighty enough for one of our discussions.

For the benefit of anyone who is less preoccupied with the happenings of my stultifying life than I am, my old, tried-and-true cable-knit sweater had disappeared from the back of my office chair and I had written a column lamenting its loss. (It's rare in this life that you can whine and get paid for it, so I try to maximize every opportunity.)

A week passed after the column appeared and the sweater was still missing. A few people actually had stopped me to ask if it had been returned, and I — with my paranoid delusions intact — had to tell them that sadly, it had not.

I virtually froze at my desk each morning. My discomfort was an excuse to bring up my missing sweater yet again, but that was cold comfort, so to speak. I refused to bring in another sweater, lest it follow the first into the unseen realm of things lost and never found.

Then came the call from, well, from "Oatsie" (not her real name.)

I pondered her question. The buttons were wooden, I told her.

There was silence. "Your sweater somehow walked over to my house," she said finally. "I'm looking at it now."

Emotions swirled about me: joy, relief, confusion.

"I have no recollection of ever borrowing it," she said several times, using the same tone that Al Gore does when discussing fund-raising.

We hashed it over. Apparently she had put it on while working one weekend, we decided, and had worn it home thinking it was her off-white cable-knit sweater, which is so very similar — except that it zips instead of buttons.

She had seen my sweater lying around her house several times but she assumed it was hers. So she left it where it was for her 312 or so cats to enjoy kneading. Each time I whimpered about my sweater, she, no doubt, was thinking, "Hey, I can't help it if you can't keep track of your sweater. I know EXACTLY where mine is."

At last, she had noticed the buttons. Realization struck, alleluia, and she had made her way to the telephone.

The sweater that was lost had been found and there was much rejoicing at my house. My faith in humankind had been renewed. My sweater had not been stolen; it had not been hidden in a conspiratorial effort to drive me mad. Simple human error had separated us from each other. Soon we would be reunited.

When I went into work the next morning, there was the letter — and the sweater. Once again I had a big lump of wool wedged behind me; once again I could roll my chair over the sleeves. Life was good.

The following week, I was out of work for a couple of days. When I returned I noticed the sweater was not on the chair, but my boss anticipated my hysteria and hurried to reassure me.

"I put your sweater in your drawer," he said. He explained that Oatsie (not her real name) had been skulking about and he had acted to prevent a recurrence of the missing-sweater fiasco. Wise man.

He probably thought that was the end of it, that I finally would shut up about the sweater. Guess he was wrong.

When Going Out,
She Prefers Dining In

I was so close to a clean getaway.

It was the second weekend in August, and because the summer has been unseasonably cool and there has been a lot of rain, I nearly had made it to Labor Day unscathed.

But this past weekend I got tripped up. As we entered my favorite restaurant, a friend spoke the sentence I had been dreading since June.

"Can we eat outside?"

My heart sank like a stale bagel. But being the kind of person I am, I rallied and said something unspeakably gracious, like "If we must."

Even the people who run the restaurant seemed stunned. "You're eating outside?" they chorused. There followed a round-robin of smiling and giggling and by the time they had ceased their harassment, I was seated across from my dining companion — outdoors.

Let me summarize my feelings about eating al fresco: You might as well roll down your windows and eat in your car.

I just don't get this fascination with dining on a porch or patio, unless it happens to be heavily screened and located about three feet from your own refrigerator.

But clearly I'm in the minority. Everywhere I go, people seem entranced by the notion of eating outdoors. Put two tables in the alley by the kitchen door and three couples will fight over them.

So there we were. Instead of occupying a roomy booth in a perfectly pleasant room with nice paintings on the wall, we instead were sharing a table the size of a checkerboard, gazing out over a strip of asphalt and watching people in tank tops walk by.

Now that it's over, I'll admit it wasn't that bad. The food stayed hot and, since there was a slight breeze, I stayed cool. I was inordinately happy to find that perspiration didn't roll down my face and drip all over my entree.

There was only one annoying bug and it wasn't anything deadly. It happened to be one of those things like a fruit fly, but smaller. You know, the ones that get right in your face and hover there while you keep swiping at them, ineffectually, until they're ready to go. Since no one else can see them, they create the impression that you're even loopier than people had suspected.

Aside from that, it was an OK dining experience. I've had much worse.

But my bias remains intact. Given a choice, I'll eat indoors, thanks.

Having established that, I'll go a step further: I'm not crazy about cookouts, either.

Taking part in a cookout to me is akin to doing a stint as a longshoreman. You lift, you tote, you put down. You lift, you tote, you put down. Somewhere in the course of all that backbreaking labor, you get a lunch break.

The cookout fun begins with rounding up food, charcoal, coolers, ice, plastic utensils, paper plates, salt and pepper, ketchup, mustard, relish, olives, pickles and a 250-pound watermelon.

You carry all this out the door, maybe down a flight of stairs, and across the grass to an appointed spot. Or, in variation 1-A of this scenario, you load it all into a car, drive somewhere, then unload it all and carry it across someone else's grass.

Then you cook food so laced with fat and cholesterol that you wouldn't even put it on the table indoors.

Along the way, there is a good possibility you will be slammed in the kidneys with the screen door, stub your toe and do a little piece of Martha Graham choreography with a bee.

Finally, you sit down on something that will leave either splinters imbedded or a lattice design embossed on your upper thighs. You eat whopping quantities of this healthful repast while bleating about the fresh air working up an appetite.

Somebody is sure to say: "Nothing like hamburgers, hot dogs, tofu burgers, chicken, etc., cooked on a grill, is there?"

And everyone is sure to nod agreement. Yup, they seem to say, munching away, nothing like charcoal and lighter fluid on a bun.

If you're really into this eating-out thing, you probably have a gas grill. This is a great concept and certainly a step up from the old charcoal style. Know what the next step up from a gas grill is? A STOVE.

Anyway, having eaten, and having daydreamed about antacids for a while, you say a little prayer you won't get salmonella from the deviled eggs that are shutting down your arteries at the moment, and you repack the car. The last step is to carry all the stuff you haven't eaten back indoors and put it away.

Some fun, huh? Now, all this may seem somewhat negative to you. But I actually find something very positive in it.

My friend didn't suggest a cookout. And there's only three more weeks til Labor Day.

66

The Humor in Notes on the Windshield

When you are looking through your windshield, you should see nothing but asphalt, grass, sky, trees and tail lights.

It should seem as if there were no glass between you and the world outside. You should see no cracks in the windshield; no dead bugs on it; no suicidal birds swooping toward it.

You should see no ice or snow piling up on it, no mist fogging it and none of those big, fat lazy raindrops sliding across it, obscuring your vision.

And you most certainly should see no paper. Except for an inspection sticker, paper on a windshield is seldom a good thing.

I don't want any coupons, fliers, brochures; political handouts, religious tracts — or parking tickets — jammed under my wiper blades, thanks.

I especially don't want to stagger back to the car pushing a supermarket cart fairly collapsing under the weight of the week's snacks, and find paper on my windshield. It's bad enough to have to wrestle five bags into a trunk that holds four without having to sweep an assortment of literature off the hood.

I also don't want to see any notes on my windshield. A note may mean that if I walk all the way around the car, I will discover something that will make my head hurt: a crumpled fender or dented door, for example.

I suppose a note under the wipers could be good news: "I found a large sum of money near your car. To claim it, call..." or "I love your car and would like to buy it for book value plus $2,000 in cash. Call me."

Possible. But not likely.

If most windshield communiqués give no cause for rejoicing, neither do they demand much attention. They need only be removed and discarded — with or without expletives.

But a friend of mine once left a windshield note designed to pique the recipients' curiosity in the short term, and to drive them nuts in the long term.

This friend was having dinner at a restaurant when a couple walked past her. She recognized them as teachers, married to each other, from the high school she attended in Connecticut.

They did not recognize her. Students tend to change more in 20 years than teachers do. The hair gets tamed, and the faces take on that world-weary look that the teachers' always had.

When this woman left the restaurant, she spotted the couple's car. Their vanity plate still bore their last name, as it had when my friend and Pebbles Flintstone were in school.

So she — my friend, not Pebbles — scribbled a note and left it on their windshield.

Now, this person is not someone given to hijinks. So I would have expected a note along the lines of: "Dear Mr. and Mrs. XX. Saw you inside but didn't want to intrude on your evening. I was in your classes in 19XX and I remember them well. I'm doing fine. Take care."

But it didn't say anything like that. Instead, it said: "Great to see you, Dick and Doris. Where have the years gone?"

That was a while ago. She figures they still occasionally discuss that note. I think the discussion goes like this:

DORIS: Remember that note left on the car? I still wonder who left it. Did you notice anyone inside the restaurant who looked at all familiar?

DICK: Nope. But it had to be a former student.

DORIS: I don't think so, dear. A student never would call us Dick and Doris. I think it was someone we taught with.

DICK: Well, why wouldn't he just say hello, damn it?

DORIS: Probably didn't want to intrude.

DICK: Another teacher would have signed the note, Doris. I'll tell you what I think. I think it was some wise guy trying to drive us crazy.

DORIS: Don't be silly, Dick. It sounded very sincere.

DICK: Sincere, my foot. It was probably that kid I had in 1969 — the one with the mouth. He lives somewhere near that restaurant — unless he's in prison, where he belongs.

DORIS: Oh shut up, Dick. Keep this up and you'll find divorce papers on the windshield.

Boy howdy. I tell you that note was inspired. I'm so impressed that I've been on the lookout for my former teachers — who fall into two groups.

One group liked and believed in me. To one of those teachers, I would have to write something boring but earnest, such as, "Thanks for everything."

Of course, that is a very small group — a group of, oh, about two.

To someone in the larger group — the teacher who tried to stuff me in a wall locker, for instance, I'd write this: "Hi. I bet you think I'm leaving this note because I hit your car. I didn't. But I wanted to."

Things Aren't As Bad As They Seem – Or Are They?

My friend was telling me today how, over the past weekend, she took four children for a walk along Lake Champlain in Vermont. One of her nieces, Emily, age 6, was carrying a long stick, as children like to do.

Halfway through their trek, Emily broke the stick. Momentarily disappointed, she said sadly, "Oh, I broke my stick."

Then, looking at the pieces in her hands, she brightened instantly.

"Now I have two," she said.

This child will have a good life. Even if she has a lousy life, she will have a good life. It's all in her point of view.

What can go wrong enough to spoil that sunny disposition?

If a boy decides at the last minute to cancel their date for the senior prom, she'll look at it as an opportunity to save money on the dress.

If she gets fired someday, she'll see it as an opportunity to get a better job.

When someone she loves dies, she'll say she is glad for the time they had together — and she'll mean it.

She is and ever will be dauntless. She has the looking-on-the-bright-side gene.

Hooray for her, I say.

Oddly enough, at about the time my friend and her little chicks were wending their way lakeside, I was standing in line at a takeout window in Springfield.

All I wanted was an iced tea and it should have taken about five minutes to get it. But there was a roadblock ahead — in the person of a girl, about 9 years old, who was waiting for a sundae.

She was cheery enough, chatting with her father, sister and grandmother, until she saw that the server had put pistachio ice cream in the sundae.

I don't know if she had ordered it that way or not. But clearly, it was not what she wanted.

She proceeded to pitch a fit to rival Scarlett O'Hara's turnip scene. She cried, she screamed, she raced away, ran back and circled us like a small aircraft. She even flung herself to the pavement, all the while moaning, "It's not fair" as if it were a refrain.

I'm not sure, but I think the skies actually darkened.

Bear in mind, this wasn't the Poor Little Match Girl, bellying up to the counter with a fistful of hard-earned pennies. It wasn't her last chance to have ice cream that day.

Speaking softly in an effort to calm her down, her grandmother offered her another kind of sundae, several kinds of sundaes, maybe even the moon, to shut her up. But it was useless.

The fact is, she wasn't sobbing because she couldn't have a sundae. She was sobbing because her will had been thwarted; her dream of a perfect sundae had been tarnished. And nothing could make up for that.

Finally, her father escorted her from the area. He didn't have to handcuff her, but I was worried for a minute.

I was thinking today that if Pistachio Girl had broken HER stick on a walk along the lake, she would have needed 15 years of therapy.

What's the difference between these two girls? Heredity? Environment? Karma? A little of all three? Who knows?

I guess we can blame Pistachio Girl's parents for her behavior. We blame parents for everything else, heaven knows. (The old movie *The Bad Seed* would be titled *The Different Seed of Dysfunctional Parents* today.)

I think it was in part that she is a cranky little girl. But my views on such matters are not always the politically correct ones. I even happen to believe there IS such a thing as a bad boy. (And he used to live down the street from me.)

I also think that these two children represent a very real division among humans: There are those who see the droppings, and those who can envision the pony.

Or, there are those who take everything personally, and those who don't.

In direct contrast to Emily, Pistachio Girl seems bound to grow up unhappy. Even if her life is good, she will complain a lot. She will cry often and loudly and will irritate even those who love her.

If she wins the lottery, she'll grouse about the taxes. If she gets promoted, she'll say the money still stinks. If someone she loves dies, she'll swear he or she did it just to make her miserable.

I suspect that when she reaches maturity, she will file many frivolous lawsuits — as adult whiners like to do.

All of that is unfortunate.

So unfortunate that even little Emily could not put a positive spin on it.

Unless, of course, she grows up to be Pistachio Girl's lawyer.

Siblings: The Advantage Is Relative

A co-worker made the nicest offer the other day: She offered to give me some of her brothers.

I was very touched, until she started setting conditions on the gift. I could have my choice of them, she said, except for her favorite — the funniest one.

That part was fine with me, since I certainly don't need any more competition.

But I decided to pass on the offer altogether when it became apparent that the brothers she was willing to give up would have done me no good at all: None of them is handy with a hammer and all of them think a loose packing has something to do with luggage.

Rest assured that I am no sexist. I gladly would have accepted a female sibling who could lend me a hand, but she didn't even put her sister on the block. This surprised me, actually, since doing so would have given her unrestricted access to her sister's closet, where she claims to spend a lot of time.

Anyway, that's her business, and it's not as if I were

entitled to any of these people. So that's pretty much that.

But the conversation got me thinking about this sibling thing.

Most only children occasionally wonder about having a big brother or a little sister — or vice versa — as they are growing up. But it's a casual thing, a vague longing, like wishing you had a pony.

You don't really expect one to appear in your front yard, and you probably wouldn't know what to do with it if one did. But it's fun to muse about. Likewise, the prospect of having siblings is pleasant to ponder.

Since life is a series of trade-offs, the lack of siblings has some distinct advantages. As an only child you have to learn to amuse yourself on rainy afternoons, and must always remember your lunch money. But, on the other hand, you get to eat all the cookies, and everything under the Christmas tree is yours.

As an adult only child, you avoid the psychological pitfalls of sibling rivalry, and everything your parents want to get rid of is yours.

But there are those moments throughout life when you wish for a genetic link to other people — people who not only would tolerate your peculiarities, but also might even mirror them.

So if I actually could order a brother or sister to specification, what would I ask for?

In a brother, it would be nice to have a sensitive man of the 90s, who could discuss women's issues and empathize with my points of view. But then, it also would be nice to have a Neanderthal who could beat the stuffing out of anyone who messed with me — or at least looked as if he could.

It's probably too much to expect all those traits in one man, isn't it?

As a bare minimum, I'd want my ideal brother to be handy — a foreign-car mechanic maybe, who did a little carpentry and plumbing on the side and loved the smell of freshly mown grass.

In a sister, it would be helpful to have someone who likes to wash dishes and gets a kick out of emptying litter boxes.

These traits are not gender-specific, of course. A brother who loved to drop over and run the vacuum and a sister who could hang a door would be dandy.

My perfect sibling — of either sex — would be generous to a fault and would have a wealthy partner who also thought I was wonderful and couldn't do enough for me. It would be a bonus if they had a child, so that I would have an excuse to see Disney movies.

In reality, of course, few people have ideal siblings. Many people have siblings they don't even like much.

Brothers and sisters can be rude, thoughtless and greedy. Friends tell me siblings sometimes rat on you, ruin your stuff and blame you for things they did. They also have been known to use a car without permission and borrow money and never repay it.

Worse yet, they may grow up to be virtual strangers with whom you disagree about everything under the sun, turning every family gathering into a homespun version of "Firing Line".

So, all things taken together, I guess I'll settle for eating all the cookies — and waiting for the pony.

Suffering the Sling of Outrageous Fortune

Each year 26.3 million Americans slip on wet leaves, fall and sprain a wrist. Of that number, some 12.1 million sprain their left wrists.

Those figures are totally bogus; I just made them up. Statistics, while unspeakably boring in my view, seem to lend an air of credibility to any story. I could look up the bona fide statistics, but I'm not feeling up to it because I fell and sprained my wrist last week.

Continuing my efforts to illuminate other lives with my tragic experiences, I would like to share my insights into the worst things associated with having one hand rendered temporarily useless.

First, a sprain, while fairly minor, forces you to hurl yourself into the maelstrom known as today's health-care system. In my case, this meant, for openers, an encounter with the triage nurse in the emergency room where I sought treatment.

It usually takes people an instant to form an instant dislike for me. In her case, it was a nanosecond. After she took my blood pressure on the affected arm, pumping up the sphygmomanometer until my sore fingers threatened to explode like pork sausages on a gas grill, she said testily, "You should take off that ring."

"I can't get it off," I said apologetically.

"Well, you should take it off," she insisted.

"I put it on 40 years and more than 40 pounds ago," I offered in an example of the witty repartee for which I am so well known.

She made one of those harumphing sounds — probably unwilling to believe I could be over 40.

"It's your decision," she said and that was that. Apparently she is adept at stating a problem but not so hot at solving one. Bad nursie.

Since I didn't have a jeweler with me, I was licked, but I am pleased to report the finger is still there and the ring is still on it.

Next stop was the X-ray department. (There's been a big push of late to refer to X-rays as radiographs. Seems kind of pretentious to me, so I try never to do it.) There, they asked me to put my hand into several positions. Had I been able to achieve any of them, I would not have gone to the ER in the first place.

Undaunted by my love fest with Ms. Triage, I dared to share that observation with the technician. She laughed. "That's because the people who write the X-ray books don't have anything wrong with them."

Not only did she have a sense of humor, but she was friendly. She'll be working in marketing soon. More money and no nights.

Once the X-ray was read, I was splinted and slinged, so to speak, and I made my weary way home — where I discovered other annoying things about having a sprained wrist. You cannot efficiently tie shoes; fasten other essential articles of clothing; open jars and cans; drain pasta; wash your hair; or change the litter box. Other people might feel the lack of other skills more keenly. This is my list.

You also cannot rid your yard of the 300,000 leaves per

square foot that have accumulated there. You could rake and bag the leaves with one hand, but it would be like moving the dunes at Truro with a bucket. I passed. There's always spring.

Another irritant is that people tend to get the story confused. One woman thought that when I said "I fell out there," I had said "I fell off my chair." As if there were not enough snide remarks being made about my coordination.

There are also the people who will tell you that a sprain is worse than a break. To me it is as if they are challenging the gods. And it is a theory I would prefer not to test, thanks.

The doctors say I'll be fine soon — and should be able to play the piano. That's remarkable because I never could... well, you know.

When Today's Neurosis
Is a Thing of the Past

In recent years I've met several people who have done past-life regressions.

I find this wholly fascinating, and have thought about doing it myself, except that it costs more than I'm willing to spend. Whatever else I may have been in my earlier incarnations, I'm willing to bet you even money that I was tight with a buck.

For the uninitiated, past-life regression involves delving into your previous existences with the aid of someone such as a psychic. He or she acts as a guide and helps you to see and understand patterns that may be at work even now in your current life.

For example, to learn that you once hobnobbed with Francis of Assisi might explain your preoccupation with the neighbor's birdfeeder and your relative lack of interest in your wardrobe. Likewise, your days aboard an ancient sailing ship may relate to your passion for salt-water taffy.

Appearances to the contrary, none of this strikes me as amusing in the least. Whether one believes in past lives or not, it's an interesting prospect. And any quest for enlightenment and fulfillment should be taken seriously, I believe.

Well, let me amend that: I cannot respect anyone who seeks meaning and contentment in a jelly doughnut. But that's only because I've tried it and know it to be sheer folly.

Fortunately, while I am too cheap to pay for my own past-life regression, I have had the opportunity to hear others recount their sessions. And I am grateful for that. It has been both entertaining and instructive.

I especially like the way people change genders and nationalities as they muddle through their multiple lives: In one century a woman may have been Cleopatra's best friend; in another, she may have been Lincoln's best man.

I take this as more proof that it really is a small world, by gum, and, as I always suspected, infinity really isn't much longer than that 45 minutes you spend in the dentist's chair.

What occurs to me, however, is that daily life, like a historical novel, seems always to be more interesting simply because it is set in a prior century.

For example, it is more exciting to learn you once sold big crusty loaves of bread off a cart in medieval England than it is to be a baker in Greenfield.

It is more provocative to learn about your steamy and sordid love affair with a nobleman in 16th-century France than it is to try to match your boyfriend's suits and ties.

And it is more thrilling to hear about your days riding the wagon train west to California than to be a trucker trying to get out of Hartford on Interstate 91.

But what will it be like for people in future centuries to learn of lives they spent here and now?

I close my eyes and imagine my session in some psychic's living room/office 200 years from today. It's a futuristic room with lots of chrome and glass. Or maybe that's the psychic's car. Anyway, she speaks:

"I see you in the late 1900s, maybe around 1980 or 90. You're working at what looks like an old television set. It's probably some kind of early computer. They refer to you as a copy editor. It is a strange job. I don't have a clear idea of what it involved. Wait. I'm getting a feeling that back then you had no clear idea of what it involved either.

"I have a sense of your being tired, and I feel that this was a chronic problem for you, just as it is in this life — this seems to be a pattern.

"It may be that you took on too many tasks, that you worked much too hard and deserved to have praise and money heaped upon you.. Or it may be that you stayed up to watch David Letterman."

Then, as I imagine the scene, the psychic would turn solemn. "I feel that in that life long ago you were a seeker of truth and wisdom. You struggled with the mysteries of life. But you often digressed and took the wrong path.

"This is clear to me,' she would intone soberly, "from the jelly spots on your shirt."

Take Two Aspirin and Call a Few Relatives

A friend told me a story the other day that makes me think I have found the poster family for health-care reform.

This incident involves three generations, and took several hours to unfold. I'll try to tell it chronologically.

It began when Shirley, a grandmother of two, began experiencing some chest pain and arrhythmia. This is no laughing matter. But she has had this in the past, and it has proved to be a matter of adjusting medication, so she did not become unduly alarmed, which probably was good.

She also did not feel the need to hurry to the hospital, which probably was bad.

Instead, she called her mother, Nanny, who is 93.

Fortunately, Nanny was at home when Shirley called. She could have been out mowing her lawn or driving her station wagon around town, or even at the dentist.

Seriously. This woman has more energy than Mary Lou Retton.

But Nanny was available and happy to run over — well, walk over; she's not that energetic — and since they live on the same street she was there in minutes.

Her job was to sit with Shirley, providing reassurance and support.

After a while, the two decided to call Shirley's daughter, Janet — but with some misgivings.

You know how the kids get when Mom is sick.

They waited until 5 p.m., when Janet's workday would be over and then called and asked her to come over because Shirley felt like a chat.

Janet — no fool, she — realized that 5 p.m. was an odd time to be invited for a chat, especially by your mother who knows perfectly well that you have a family to feed. So she raced over, suspecting there was something amiss.

When she arrived, she found Shirley and Nanny at the kitchen table eating hot dogs and beans.

Now, if I were experiencing a little chest discomfort, I might still want to eat. God knows, nothing else stops me. But I somehow doubt that hot dogs and beans would be my meal of choice.

However, nobody made me official menu planner, so it's none of my business.

Shirley admitted to Janet that she was having a little discomfort, prompting Janet to wonder aloud: "Then what the hell are you doing sitting here eating hot dogs and beans?"

Her mother and grandmother exchanged a look. "That's why I didn't want to call her," Shirley said to Nanny. "I knew she'd get upset."

Immediately, Janet began putting on the pressure for a trip to the emergency room. Staunchly, Shirley resisted.

She just didn't want to go. She'd just been there a week or two earlier. She was sick of the place. I suspect she also didn't want to be a bother.

They argued — Janet trying to win her point without making her mother sicker; Shirley just trying to enjoy her beans, for Pete's sake.

Janet decided to call for backup. She telephoned

Shirley's sister, Betty, a school nurse who lives about 15 minutes away.

Betty encouraged, cajoled, demanded that Shirley go to the ER.

Nope. No way. No how.

Betty then got in her car and drove down to Shirley's house, with her stethoscope and gave a listen to her sister's ticker. Then she said even more sternly: "Shirl, you have to go to the hospital."

Shirley was not to be persuaded.

Then Betty brought out the big guns. "I'm calling Bob," she said.

At this point in the story, people invariably ask, "Who's Bob?" I did.

Well, as it turns out, Bob is a nephew of Shirley's. But more importantly, he is an ambulance driver.

(Here I would like to note that no one to this point has requested a physician's services. The case has been handled entirely by allied health-care professionals. That course may have been a tad risky in this particular case, but it represented a valiant attempt to minimize care and keep costs down, wouldn't you agree?)

Back to the story: Bob was called for a consultation and concurred in the finding that the emergency room was the place for Shirley.

Shirley still said no.

Then Bob, a student of psychology if ever there was one, said, "If you don't go right now, I'm going to come down there and make you go in the ambulance."

That did it.

"Well, OK," she said, her desire to remain low profile greater than her reluctance to bother the ER people.

She went; she's home; she's fine, which to me, proves two things: Prompt medical attention is vital, but there's no substitute for a caring family.

And when you're feeling a little puny, you just can't beat a good dish of beans.

Advice Can Be More Trouble Than It's Worth

I'd like to offer two rules about advice.

Rule No. 1: When seeking advice, the only people you should seek it from are the people who will tell you what you want to hear.

Rule No. 2: When giving advice, remember Rule No. 1 and act accordingly.

These are simple rules, but adhering to them can spare you a lot of wear and tear. Let me offer an example.

You back out of a high driveway and bang your car's undercarriage on the concrete. You bang it hard enough to loosen your back teeth, so you're worried. You get out and crawl around the car on your hands and knees. You have no idea what you're looking for, of course, but it seems the thing to do.

There are no gaping holes, no hanging exhaust pipes. But there's still that nagging anxiety.

Clearly, it's time to ask for some advice.

So you mosey up to the acknowledged car expert in the workplace, being careful to appear neutral. You don't want to influence his reaction by communicating panic.

"Hit my undercarriage today," you say casually. "Think that did any harm?"

"That depends," he responds. Then he adds, "Chances are you have a skid pad."

Here you decide it's best to nod and shrug at the same time, as if to say, "Hey, who doesn't?"

"If the steering seems OK and the car doesn't drift, it's probably all right," he concludes. Then he goes back to work.

A little later you put the same questions to a friend. "I've done that lots of times," she says. "Nothing bad happens. Don't worry about it."

Now, who do you think gave the better advice? Let's look closely.

In the case of the car expert, you're grateful mostly for the advice he did NOT give: He didn't tell you to hang a "for sale" sign on the car and walk home. So you feel a little better. But he has given you implied advice: Keep an eye on the car's steering.

This plays on your neuroses. For the next 48 hours, you will think you detect a wobble, a pull to the right, or maybe to the left. You'll have to fight the urge to take your hands off the wheel while traveling 55 just to see if the car drifts.

Obviously he knows what he's talking about, and your friend doesn't know a skid pad from a hole in the ground. Not important, I say.

Some people may prefer informed, enlightened counsel.

Not me. I want platitudes. And so do most people, I think.

Here's another example — this one from the viewpoint of the advice giver. A woman tells you what a lout her companion is. You listen carefully. Your integrity demands that you tell her the truth. "Dump the stiff," you say. You give her 10 good reasons why. She listens. She cries. She thanks you.

Two days later, she and the boyfriend are linking pinkies over a plate of burritos and neither of them is speaking to you.

So much for your good advice.

What could you have said to her instead? Three possibilities have merit.

A. I'm sorry, I don't speak English.

B. Yes, he is a fool and a reprobate, but he wears nice ties and I can understand why you can't bear to leave him.

C. I wouldn't touch this one with a 10-foot pole. Let's all go out for burritos.

The best answer is B. It allows you to confirm her assessment of the situation and express your own low opinion of the bum while covering yourself nicely in case of a reconciliation.

(Answer C. is also a good one, but only if you like burritos.)

The fact is that the woman only wanted to vent her spleen. She didn't want or need your advice. She hated your advice. And now she may hate you.

There are two valuable lessons here.

First, when approached to give advice, refrain. If anyone even begins a sentence with "I need your advice," flee as though running from molten lava. If necessary, move away and make a new friend. You're about to lose that one anyway.

On the flip side, when tempted to solicit advice, refrain. Never begin a sentence with, "I need your advice." The advice you get probably will make you feel worse. Say instead, "I need you either to agree with me or make soothing noises," since that's what you're really after.

I think most of us should develop our own problem-solving abilities anyway.

Don't ask me how.

These Arrangements Remain Incomplete

A friend of mine wrote several articles for a funeral and estate planning guide. It made her some fun to be around. Nothing like a good debate on the relative merits of burial vs. cremation to get the conversational ball rolling.

Actually, journalists are known for this. They gather a lot of information about a particular subject, share it with everyone they know while planning the article, then write it and promptly move on to the next topic.

So it was not surprising that while covering what I refer to as the "death and taxes beat," my friend turned into quite the expert. She became especially enthusiastic about preplanning and prepaying one's funeral and has been urging me to do that.

She notes the financial benefits and the fact that it will spare my survivors an unpleasant task, as if I care. She also points out that I could pretty much design the funeral I want, instead of leaving it to someone who may choose to dress me in crinoline petticoats for all eternity.

True, but there is something about the idea that makes

me uncomfortable, and I've been a little resistant. Well, maybe more than a little. I think my response was something akin to "Plan your own damn funeral, why don't you?"

I was concerned that what I planned and paid for might be as final as my demise. We all go through stages in our lives, and the funeral I might plot out today may not be the funeral I would want tomorrow. At the age of 14, I would have wanted a picture of Pat Boone in my casket. Need I say more?

One day I might want an opulent funeral with a sit-down dinner and an open bar for my friends. The next I might opt for a reading of Buddhist texts over a plain wooden coffin.

In fact, I read about a man who makes caskets that can double as furniture until they are pressed into service. That appeals to me this year, but by next year I may want said plain casket encased in kryptonite. The idea of becoming one with the earth has a certain ecological appeal in the abstract but we are, after all, talking about MY remains.

When I laid out these arguments, so to speak, my friend rolled her eyes. "It's not as if they put your name on a casket and stick it in the back room for 40 years, Pam," she said. "You buy $5,000 worth of services, for example, and how that $5,000 is spent when the time comes is up to your survivors."

What a relief.

I had held a picture in my mind of my executor saying to the funeral director, "We've decided we would like someone to sing 'Ave Maria,'" and the FD looking pained and saying ever so patiently but firmly, "I'm terrible sorry. Ms. Robbins did not mention anything about 'Ave Maria' and there will be no 'Ave Maria' at the funeral. Perhaps you could work out something with the caterer."

"Surely, we could find some place to add the 'Ave Maria,'" my executor would say incredulously.

"No we most assuredly could not," I imagined the FD replying. "Ms. Robbins ordered our blue-plate special. No substitutions allowed. Had she chosen to, she could have had our a la carte plan. But she balked at the additional cost. I know because I was there when my grandfather made her arrangements MANY, MANY years ago."

Since my friend convinced me that this scenario would not occur, I have felt more open to the prepaid-funeral notion and have been considering it quite seriously.

Meanwhile, another woman I know offered a comment that suggests a twist on the original premise — and a golden marketing opportunity for funeral directors everywhere.

"I've been planning my mother-in-law's funeral ever since I got married," she said.

For Healthiest Holiday Eating, Omit the Food

It seems that everywhere I turn, someone is telling me how to prepare a bountiful holiday feast that is low in fat, low in cholesterol and low in calories. Oh, and delicious, of course. They always add that.

I've been trying to remember everything I hear and read so that I can plan my holiday menu, but I'm not much of a cook and my mind is getting muddled.

However, I think I have the gist of it and I'd like to share it with those who have concerns about their health and appearance. These are only highlights. Better recipes — the kind that list actual ingredients and amounts — can be found in any cookbook, which this clearly is not.

Anyway, I have compiled this list of popular dishes for you to consider serving this holiday:

Low-fat, low-cholesterol, low-calorie turkey:
Buy a turkey and bring it home, trying not to slip a disc lifting it out of the trunk. Cook turkey on rack in oven until it's done. Take skin off turkey and give it to the cat or

dog, so someone in the house will enjoy this meal. Serve small, dry portion of white meat on big plate.

Diet stuffing:

Mix pieces of bread with eggs and spices. You'll probably need some liquid, too, I forget. Then cook it. You can stuff your turkey with it, unless you've read 700 articles about salmonella. In that case, serve it on the side.

Ultra-diet stuffing:

For those on really strict diets, use recipe above, but omit eggs. For those on killer diets, also omit bread and just mix spice and liquid together. Ladle the result over the dry white turkey on the plate.

Vegetable medley:

I love that word, medley. It conjures up a picture of happy, humming vegetables. If you don't like your vegetables all mushed together, and you have a complete set of pots and pans and about 11 burners on your stove, you can cook separate ones. Suggestions include squash, carrots, turnips, sweet potatoes and Brussels sprouts, although Brussels sprouts never seem festive enough to me.

You can boil the vegetables or steam them or bake them. But remember: Do not add butter, do not add salt. Just serve vegetables in big bowls and let guests pile them on their plates, next to the dry turkey.

Important note: When preparing vegetables, do not add little white marshmallows to anything. In general, avoid recipes that include the words glazed and candied.

Low-cal gravy:

Scrape up all the drippings glued to the bottom of the pan you cooked the turkey in. Throw them in the garbage. They make the gravy worth eating, but they also make it very fattening. Boil some water in the pan, add spices left over from the low-cal stuffing (see above) and stir. Add flour to thicken — or don't. If you're serious about your diet, omit gravy and just ladle more ultra-diet stuffing (see above) onto the dry turkey.

Low-cal cranberry sauce:
Buy those fresh berries in the plastic bag. Don't try to cut them with a knife because they will ricochet around the kitchen and injure you severely. Either crunch them up in a food processor or pound them with a big hammer. Then cook them until they are soft enough to eat. Some people like to add sugar, but I think that's a mistake if you're on a diet. Suit yourself.

Diet pie:
Buy or make a pie, any kind, although I favor pumpkin. Mincemeat is OK, I guess, but it looks like something that should be a main course.

If you are limiting your fat and calories, eat just the filling and only a little of it. If you are seriously dieting, offer your piece of pie to the dog or cat: It should be done eating the turkey skin by then, although it probably should not eat pie either.

White wine:
I'm not sure what you're supposed to do with this. I think you can baste your turkey with it, which will make it less dry, I guess, unless it's dry wine. The man who told me this is a chef and he said to use table wine instead of cooking wine. So, I guess if you like wine, you better buy a bottle for yourself and a bottle for the turkey. So to speak.

NOTE: Don't try to substitute club soda for white wine. It works fine in awkward social situations, but it's terrible for cooking.

There Are Aisles to Go Before We Sleep

Oh boy, it's only four more days until Christmas. I'm so excited I hardly can stand it — but not for the reasons you might think.

Sure, I like getting a gift or two — or 20 — and I always enjoy a few hundred cards, but those aren't the reasons I'm so excited.

What thrills and delights me is the knowledge that once Dec. 25 rolls around, I won't have to go into another department or discount store for months.

Yes, Virginia, there are people who hate to shop, and I'm one of them. In my opinion, any task so demanding and time-consuming should involve benefits and a retirement plan.

I've hated shopping since I was a small child, but I hate it much more now that I can't lie down on the carpeted floor when I get tired. Well, I can, but chances are someone would call security.

I look at my calendar and tell myself we're in the home stretch now. This should comfort me, but I fear I'll snap at the last minute. If I do manage to make it to the big day without running amok in a mall, the credit will go to my repressive New England upbringing.

These are the things I hate most about Christmas shopping:

The store situation. There are too many stores to visit. If you should happen to fall in with the wrong crowd, i.e., with people who actually enjoy shopping, you conceivably could spend the entire holiday season on an escalator.

The lose-lose situation. When shopping for gifts, you lose time and money up front, obviously. But then you lose again when the person for whom you have done the shopping either hates the gift, loves the gift but finds it doesn't fit, or has the same thing in beige.

The other-shoppers situation. There are too many shoppers and they all drive cars, so just getting into and out of the parking lots is a challenge.

Inside the stores, the other shoppers insist on trying to occupy the space I'm in at the moment I'm in it. They jostle me and encourage their children to stomp on my insteps. They never say "excuse me" or get out of the way to accommodate me, although it's clear that they enjoy being at the mall and I don't. You'd think they would take that into consideration, wouldn't you?

The box situation. This has been the worst part of shopping this year. Is there a global box shortage or something?

Stores used to give you nice boxes when you bought nice gifts. They were boxes with gumption that could withstand my clumsy wrapping efforts. Now the stores that give boxes at all give you flimsy things, not much sturdier than the tissue paper inside them — which also is getting pretty sparse, by the way.

One store this year really sandbagged me. After I spent $76 on their stupid stuff, all of which will be exchanged within 24 hours after being exclaimed over, I asked about boxes.

"Yes, we have boxes," the woman said merrily. "They cost a dollar each. But you get the wrapping paper and the bow."

I didn't want wrapping paper and a bow. I have enough wrapping paper and bows at home to wrap the Space Shuttle Columbia. I didn't ask for either. I asked for a box.

I looked around me. This store actually had signs fluttering above some racks of hideous clothing that said, "Buy one, get one free." But they couldn't give me a free box? Something seemed wrong with that picture.

I said no thanks to the boxes, and was pretty snippy about it, too.

Of course, having taken such a firm stand, I'm forced to spend these last gala days rummaging around the house, looking for past years' boxes for this year's gifts.

Maybe I'll skip the boxes and just wrap the items in cheery paper. That's what the Ingalls family always did on "Little House on the Prairie." And they always seemed to have such wonderful holidays.

But then, why wouldn't they? There was only one store in town.

Plummeting Into Those Golden Years

I came across a story from the Associated Press earlier this month that caught my eye. The suggested headline, put on by someone at the wire service, was: "Woman observes 90th birthday with parachute jump."

I couldn't wait to read it. I always am amazed by stories like this. I think anyone who does something adventurous at the age of 90 is remarkable.

To be honest, I think anyone who does anything adventurous at any age is wonderful. Adventure to me means anything more daring than starting the week's grocery shopping at the other end of the supermarket.

However, I must admit that I'm torn. On the one hand, I am moved and inspired by those who take risks, go out on a limb, push the envelope. But on the other, I never will understand in my heart of hearts why a person — of any age — would jump out of a plane voluntarily — unless the engines were on fire.

I read on, eager to learn more, and discovered that

Merita Welch of West Carrollton, Ohio, had decided at age 85 that she would do the sky dive "if God let me live to 90."

Right there I knew this woman and I were different kinds of people — polar opposites, really.

If God let ME live to see 90, for example, I would stay home and keep very still. I would not do anything to attract his attention — in the fervent hope that he would forget I was there and let me live to see 91.

Still, Merita Welch deserves congratulations not only for her courage and her joie de vivre, but also for her remarkable skeletal structure, which miraculously remained intact. Some serious calcium consumption must have gone on in her family.

For anyone not awestruck by her feat already, there was more. The reporter who wrote the story about her went on to say:

Although she had just recovered from pneumonia, Welch — who is 4-foot-10 and weighs 94 pounds — said her only concern was that she might damage her expensive plastic hip and knee.

"I wasn't scared a bit," she said.

To make a short story shorter, this woman took a little lesson at the local sky-diving emporium, hugged her family and friends— always a good idea before you freefall several thousand feet — then made a "tandem jump." In other words, an experienced jumper controlled the action, and she hung on.

"Oh, it was just great," she said later. "I'd do it again."

Pneumonia; 94 pounds; not afraid? Again it was clear to me that Welch and I would not hit it off. She'd no doubt write me off as an old stick-in-the-mud.

And rightly so. My idea of a high time is dinner and a movie, and I think that if we were meant to jump from planes, we would come equipped with landing gear.

I wonder what this incredible woman will do her next birthday — scale the Matterhorn? Swim the English Channel? Cross diagonally at a major intersection?

Whatever it is, I'll be keeping an eye out for the news story. I know there will be one. Media types just can't resist this stuff.

Meanwhile, I'll also be keeping close tabs on similar and related articles — all the ones about how very old people explain their longevity.

I think young and middle-age people read these stories in the same spirit that they explore various diet and exercise regimens. We're all still looking for the magic elixir.

But the information passed on by the elders can be confusing. It seems no two nonagenarians ever agree.

Some say they never drink or smoke and brag about their clean living. Others gloat that they knock off a pint of bourbon every day and smoke a big cigar to boot.

For every woman who has walked 10 miles daily since puberty, there's another who has sat in a rocker since 1958. If there's one 100-year-old who has eaten no meat for 70 years, there's another who tucks away a slab o' beef nightly — with a side of fried eggs and a stack of buttered toast for a chaser.

It's all so baffling.

Personally, I've always identified with another elderly woman — the subject of an AP story out of Boston in January of 1990.

While I didn't make note of her name, I identified with this woman so strongly that I filed a couple of paragraphs from the piece about her.

This 104-year-old was asked, of course, to what she attributed her long life.

"I just try to go along and not lift anything heavy," she told reporters.

Seems like sage advice to me.

You Bet
I Can Spend It

Years ago, when the Massachusetts state lottery began, people used to spend a lot of time ruminating about what they would do if they won. I don't hear people doing that much anymore unless the jackpot is enormous.

Nobody seems to get excited about the prospects of winning a mere $500,000 or a million. They want to talk about $7 million or $11 million.

Not me. I would be excited about a half-million, a quarter-million, even a measly $50,000.

I must admit, however, that one needs to tailor the spending plan to the amount of anticipated prize money. No sense planning to outfit a yacht if you're only going to be able to buy a rowboat.

Being someone who likes to have a plan in place beforehand — I'd prepay my funeral if I really believed I was going to die someday — I have listed below some lottery winnings, and how I would spend them.

$1 to $100. Buy more tickets.

$100 to $500. Buy lunch for all the people I like. Since

I don't like many people, $100 could do it and $500 surely would.

$500 to $1,000. Buy dinner for people mentioned above. (Might have to do this in increments because some of the people I like don't like each other.)

$1,000 to $10,000. Put some money in bank; think about buying a new car. If I decide against buying new car, get this car washed.

Also buy presents for close personal friends; don't believe everyone who says he or she is my close personal friend.

$10,000 to $25,000. Go look at new cars, late-model used cars; keep current car; put money in bank.

$25,000 to $50,000. Buy new or newer car; hire someone to wash all the windows in the house; think about some new appliances; give all the people I like gift certificates so they can go to dinner without me because I will be too busy managing my newfound wealth.

Also, ask to cut my hours at work. If they say yes, watch more TV; if they say no, think about quitting altogether.

$50,000 to $100,000. Do all of the above plus hire someone to take care of the yard; fill an entire order form in the L.L. Bean catalog even if I have to send all the stuff back, and to hell with how much the shipping and handling fees cost.

Also, give my friend who likes to travel a trip, a short trip; give my friend with the house that needs painting enough money to paint the house. Well, think about that one, anyway.

And, give a month's notice at work and offer to fill in if they ever need me.

$100,000 to $250,000. Do everything listed above except give only two weeks notice and skip the offer to fill in; think about buying a new house; resolve to pay someone to do my typing forevermore.

$250,000 to $1 million. Give 10 minutes notice, then clear out my desk and throw its contents into the trash can; go home to count my money and watch TV round the clock.

Also, call several real estate agents and tell them I have a big fat wad of cash and want a new house in a hurry. Then watch them scramble.

Also, go ahead and have my friend's house painted; take people I don't like all that much to dinner if they have ever even once been nice to me, because I am rich and they are not.

Also; buy a new house; park my new car outside it and eat take-out food for a really long time.

$1 million on up. Take all the people I have ever worked with in my entire life out to dinner. Laugh when they talk about retiring.

Also, look at photos of my traveler friend's trip; admire my other friend's freshly painted house; feel guilty about doing nothing and resolve to volunteer for some worthwhile cause. Right after the New Year.